"Times-a-changing!—'Ole time religion' or old ways of doing church are no longer sufficient. Dan Kreiss and Efrem Smith are keen to note the need for faith that brings people together. This book is a must-read for anyone concerned about building unifying communities of faith more than divisive institutions of faith."

Antipas L. Harris, founder, president, and dean of the Urban Renewal Center in Norfolk, Virginia, and author of *Is Christianity the White Man's Religion?*

"Here is just the book for our present moment: an enlivening vision of a church that nourishes life in its fullness, fosters true relationships between diverse people, and brings us closer to the God who loves us all. May we hear and heed this call to hope."

Karen Wright Marsh, author of *Vintage Saints and Sinners* and *Wake Up to Wonder*

"I wholeheartedly endorse *Church for Everyone* by Dan Kreiss and Efrem Smith. As regional president of Converge PacWest, I have witnessed the challenge of attracting and retaining emerging young adults in faith communities that lack inclusiveness, social justice, racial reconciliation, and multiracial representation. *Church for Everyone* is an essential read for pastors, leaders, and individuals who are passionate about creating vibrant, diverse, and justice-oriented faith communities. Through their profound insights, Kreiss and Smith inspire hope and provide a road map for those seeking to navigate the challenges and seize the opportunities of our increasingly diverse world."

Bernard Emerson, regional president of Converge PacWest

DAN
KREISS

AND

EFREM
SMITH

CHURCH FOR EVERYONE

BUILDING A MULTI-INCLUSIVE
COMMUNITY FOR EMERGING
GENERATIONS

ivp

An imprint of InterVarsity Press
Downers Grove, Illinois

InterVarsity Press
P.O. Box 1400 | Downers Grove, IL 60515-1426
ivpress.com | email@ivpress.com

InterVarsity Press® is the publishing division of InterVarsity Christian Fellowship/USA®. For more information, visit intervarsity.org.

All Scripture quotations, unless otherwise indicated, are taken from The Holy Bible, New International Version®, NIV®. Copyright © 1973, 1978, 1984, 2011 by Biblica, Inc.™ Used by permission of Zondervan. All rights reserved worldwide. www.zondervan.com. The "NIV" and "New International Version" are trademarks registered in the United States Patent and Trademark Office by Biblica, Inc.™

Scripture quotations marked MSG are taken from The Message, copyright © 1993, 2002, 2018 by Eugene H. Peterson. Used by permission of NavPress. All rights reserved. Represented by Tyndale House Publishers.

While any stories in this book are true, some names and identifying information may have been changed to protect the privacy of individuals.

Published in association with the literary agency of Mark Oestreicher.

The publisher cannot verify the accuracy or functionality of website URLs used in this book beyond the date of publication.

Cover design: David Fassett
Interior design: Daniel van Loon
Cover image: © tomograf / Getty Images

ISBN 978-1-5140-0550-7 (print) | ISBN 978-1-5140-0551-4 (digital)

Printed in the United States of America ♾

Library of Congress Cataloging-in-Publication Data
Names: Kreiss, Dan, 1965- author. | Smith, Efrem (Efrem D.), 1969- author.
Title: Church for everyone : building a multi-inclusive community for
     emerging generations / Dan Kreiss and Efrem Smith.
Description: Downers Grove, IL : IVP, [2024] | Includes bibliographical
     references.
Identifiers: LCCN 2023037070 (print) | LCCN 2023037071 (ebook) | ISBN
     9781514005507 (paperback) | ISBN 9781514005514 (ebook)
Subjects: LCSH: Church. | Race relations–Religious aspects–Christianity.
     | Cultural pluralism–Religious aspects–Christianity.
Classification: LCC BV600.3 .K745 2024 (print) | LCC BV600.3 (ebook) |
     DDC 262.001/7–dc23/eng/20231003
LC record available at https://lccn.loc.gov/2023037070
LC ebook record available at https://lccn.loc.gov/2023037071

29   28   27   26   25   24 | 12   11   10   9   8   7   6   5   4   3   2   1

DAN

For all the students with whom I have had the pleasure to work—Youth for Christ Wellington, Knox Presbyterian Church, Hutt International Boys' School, King University, and Roswell Presbyterian Church—this is for you and those like you around the world.

EFREM

For the Midtown Church family: I am honored to copastor a church that is truly for everyone. I specifically want to give a shoutout to founding pastor, Bob Balian, and colead pastor, Susie Gamez. I'm grateful to team with you both. Finally, for my wife, Donecia, and daughters, Jaeda and Mireya.

CONTENTS

INTRODUCTION

HAILEY WAS RAISED in a traditional church setting within a Christian family and developed a genuine faith of her own. However, upon graduation she decided to move away to attend university and has become increasingly involved in activities in her new school.

Hailey has particularly enjoyed connecting with people of diverse ethnicities and cultures that were a limited part of her experiences previously. They've opened her up to new perspectives and raised some questions about her own faith. She has also become involved in various social justice initiatives at her college and is increasingly passionate about injustice toward groups of people she feels are mistreated or misunderstood. When she goes home, she shares what she's been learning and her involvement with these movements, but she's been dismayed to discover that many in her church are not appreciative of her new perspectives. She senses that most people are comfortable as they are, and they aren't overly concerned with what she feels are crucial issues for her generation. She feels more and more discontent with her home church, and she hasn't found one near her school that reflects both the diversity and the broad-mindedness she is discovering on campus.

Discouraged, she begins to distance herself from the faith of her youth, believing that she may have outgrown the monocultural community that appears to her to embrace a narrow-minded perspective. She realizes that many of her friends who had been active in youth activities with her have also lost interest in most of what the church has to offer. With little sense that her previous faith experience has much connection with her new perspective, and with a developing desire to embrace a community that offers greater opportunity for diverse relationships, she removes herself from any traditional faith community, choosing instead to pursue the new communities available to her in college.

Hailey's experience demonstrates one of the key issues undermining the commitment of young adults to Christian faith communities. They frequently perceive a lack of inclusiveness and concern for issues of social justice. A growing number of young adults are disengaging from traditional Christian faith communities and many are eliminating any consistent faith practice altogether. Those in emerging generations, across the theological and social spectrum, are responding to their perceptions of what they believe the church represents. This often occurs by removing themselves from communities of faith altogether.

* * *

Both in terms of the number of adherents and its cultural influence, the church is in freefall in the United States. Kara Powell, director of the Fuller Youth Institute and researcher on the effectiveness of the church, says that regardless of theology, geographic location, or denominational ties, "no major Christian tradition is growing in the US today."[1] The numbers are staggering and continue to grow, affecting both the Catholic and Protestant traditions.

The most recent data coming out of the Pew Research Center shows that in the past ten years the percentage of those self-identifying as Catholic declined from 23 percent to 20 percent while Protestants declined from 51 percent to 43 percent.[2] In addition, other Pew Research information indicates that although Christianity is by far the largest religion, the overall net flow in the

United States has resulted in millions moving from Christianity to "unaffiliated." Pew finds:

> Over the past 15 years the share of U.S. adults who identify as Christians (of all varieties, combined) has dropped 15 percentage points, from 78% to 63%. The share who are "nones" has grown commensurately—rising by 1 point per year, on average, from 16% to nearly 30%.[3]

It seems certain that the church is in trouble and in the midst of a membership drop off from which there is little respite. This numeric decline has been happening since the 1960s, though more notice has been taken of late because of the apparent change in attitude of emerging generations toward organized religion.

But it doesn't have to be that way—as a personal story suggests. In 2003, my wife, Donecia, and I (Efrem), along with twenty-two others, set out to plant Sanctuary Covenant Church in the Near North community of Minneapolis, Minnesota. The original vision that I believe God gave me for this church was to create a Christ-centered community for the hip-hop generation in a North Minneapolis community that was 68 percent African American. I also had a passion for racial reconciliation that went all the way back to the moment I gave my life to Christ as a teenager at an outreach event, after hearing a message from Dr. John Perkins.

Dr. Perkins, who almost lost his life during the civil rights movement in Mississippi, is a prophetic voice for racial reconciliation and righteousness, biblical justice, and Christian community development. The summer before my junior year in high school, my heart was transformed by his sermon on God's heart for unity, justice, and the dismantling of racism. Until that point, I had spent most of my life in a predominantly African American church. As a member of the hip-hop generation, I watched many of my African American friends leave the church or never attend at all. So, when I sensed a call to church planting, I had both a passion for racial reconciliation and reaching the emerging generation of unchurched African Americans.

I was not surprised that Sanctuary Covenant Church began as a multiethnic church. I was shocked, though, by the number of young White college students and young families who became part of our church. I still vividly remember our grand opening worship service in the auditorium of Minneapolis's Patrick Henry High School. I was standing next to Donecia backstage before the service began, peeking through the curtain like a kid before a school play. I noticed a lot of White people sitting throughout the auditorium. I had preached and shared the vision of the church at a couple of large White suburban churches that supported our church plant financially, so I wasn't surprised that some White people came to this grand opening service. But I was surprised that there were so many!

"Look at all these White people!" I said to Donecia.

"What are you going to do if they all come back next week?" she asked me.

Before I could answer, she had answered her own question: "You're going to be their pastor."

Week after week, as our church grew, more young White families came. I would soon get to know young married couples like Cory and Betsy, Jeremy and Sarah, and Jeremiah and Vanessa. They would become part of our worship and media teams. Jeremy would eventually come on staff as our communications and productions coordinator. Within the first year, our church grew to over five hundred in attendance and, though multiethnic, was close to 60 percent White. I never compromised being my full African American self in preaching and occasionally singing in our worship services. Once a month we had a hip-hop worship service. Our week-to-week praise and worship sound for the most part was of the urban contemporary gospel genre. And yet, we had a growing population of young White adults committing to our church.

They weren't just coming to our church, though. They were teachers, social workers, nonprofit executives, and new residents in a predominantly African American and underresourced urban community. They were no longer interested in their parents' and grandparents' predominantly White evangelical or mainline church. Nor were they interested in their politics. They wanted a diverse community—diverse church—and they desired to address the social challenges of the city. They wanted something beyond the predominantly White, suburban, upper-middle-class megachurch that had its foundation in the White flight of the 1950s, '60s, and '70s. They wanted to be a part of a faith community that didn't avoid talking about race, systemic racism, and the biblical call to justice. This emerging migration toward the multiethnic and urban church wasn't just unique to Minneapolis. Something was beginning to change in the church in the United States.

Now, almost twenty years later, I copastor a large, center-city, multiethnic church in Sacramento, California, called Midtown Church. It's one of the fastest-growing, multiethnic, multicampus, and metropolitan churches in the Western region of the United States. In just eleven years it has realized great ethnic and racial diversity. During this multiethnic flourishing, there is an opportunity for this large church to move from being a diverse congregation to a reconciling church that equips and releases crosscultural, reconciling, and justice-oriented disciple makers.

Through its core value of being a community of hope, health, and healing, Midtown Church is reaching the homeless, providing support to those in recovery from addiction, and resourcing a summer school for under-performing students in the areas of math and reading. The church has also recently been a central meeting place for forums on race, diversity, and justice.

Midtown Church has an average weekend attendance of three thousand, and its demographic breakdown is 30 percent White, 30 percent Black, 20 percent Hispanic, 10 percent Asian, and the rest a mix of other ethnicities.[4] It is in the Midtown community of Sacramento, California, an ever-increasing multiethnic and multicultural community. The Midtown community is in the shadow of downtown Sacramento and the state capitol building. In 2002 Sacramento was named the most diverse city in America by the Civil Rights Project at Harvard University.[5] The population demographic is 45 percent White, 26.9 percent Hispanic, 18.3 percent Asian, and 14.6 percent Black.[6] Last year, Midtown Church launched a second campus in the first ring suburb of Elk Grove. As with many cities in the country, first ring suburbs are becoming more urban and more ethnically diverse.

The Midtown community of Sacramento is also experiencing gentrification. It is quite normal to see homelessness and other scenes of urban poverty on one block and see hipster coffee shops and new housing developments a few blocks later. At Midtown Church, our desire as a church is not just to continue to grow as a "sneak preview of heaven" in our multiethnic diversity, but to also unleash reconciliation, compassion, and justice, as well as facilitate individual and systemic transformation in our surrounding multicultural and urban community as it struggles with disparities across race, class, and place. The hope is that our church will be a transformative asset in the Midtown community and beyond. With these focuses, we have drawn a significant population of young White college students and young families.

What we experienced in Minneapolis at the beginning of the twenty-first century is becoming a reality across the nation. It's not simply the next church fad. We must ask ourselves, "What does this mean? Is this pointing to a larger reality within the body of Christ that we must wrestle with?"

These two stark examples might serve to both help us understand some of the issues and discern some possible responses to the disengagement of those in emerging generations. They also may provide some explanations for the rapid rise of those who media outlets have labeled the "nones," and the implications that a still majority-segregated church has on their willingness to disengage from traditional Christian faith communities.

These two examples show that inclusiveness, social justice, and multiethnicity are important to many of those in emerging generations. They represent a critical and unique generation in the history of the world. The church must understand what makes them unique—with what issues they are concerned—and discern what will encourage them to reengage with the church to continue its ministry with ever greater inclusiveness.

* * *

We also must take seriously what occurred in 2020, following the death of George Floyd in Minneapolis by the knee and body weight of police officer Derek Chauvin. The protests that followed went far beyond what had been seen as a movement of mostly angry, grieved, and activist African Americans with some allies. A truly global protest movement including Whites, Asians, and Hispanics was shown on news stations. Young White men and women were highly visible in protests, on social media, and on podcasts. They showed solidarity with the Black Lives Matter movement and called out a conservative evangelicalism that was slow or totally silent when it came to providing a biblical call to justice amid George Floyd and so many other unarmed African Americans dying at the hands of police. They saw the deep irony of armed White young men going into churches and schools taking lives and being arrested by police officers, not shot and killed by them.

Some of these emerging justice-oriented young Whites were drifting away from the predominantly White and suburban evangelical churches of their parents and grandparents and finding new community in multiethnic, urban, missional, and justice-oriented churches. Others were leaving the church altogether. It raises the question, Are predominantly White evangelical churches that lack a biblical framework and ministry praxis for justice and diversity vulnerable to losing a significant portion of the younger generation? Or will this limit their ability to evangelize and make disciples within the demographic of younger unchurched Whites? Or both?

This book is about the Christian church and the emerging generations. But which segment of the Christian church are we talking about? And who exactly are these "emerging generations"? The authors of this book have experience in the African American church, the predominantly White suburban evangelical church, and the evangelical, multiethnic, and urban church. We both have studied, written about, and experienced either the exodus of young adults from the churches of their parents and grandparents or their coming into multiethnic, justice-oriented, and urban churches. Much of this book will focus on that. But a couple of things should be mentioned.

First, when referring to emerging generations, there are generalizations being made. It is fair to say that while we believe most young people seek more diverse, inclusive, and justice-oriented communities, they do not represent the whole. As we have seen in places like Charlottesville and Richmond, Virginia; Minneapolis, Minnesota; Seattle, Washington; Paris, France; and London, England, there were protests and counterprotests. Young adults were on both sides of these situations and others like them. Political divisions, polarization, and tendencies toward exclusion are evident throughout society, regardless of age. But we strongly believe that we are talking about a significant segment of emerging generations looking for diverse, representative, justice-oriented churches. This makes it worthy of our study and efforts to understand the trends that exist.

Second, this isn't the first time emerging generations have cared about faith and justice. During the civil rights movement of the 1950s and '60s, White college students in the North risked their lives by getting on freedom buses and into cars to venture down

South to confront the injustice of the Jim Crow system. Also, today's emerging generations are more ethnically and racially diverse than previous generations. While the "nones" may conjure images of hipster, Caucasian young adults, this trend is not limited to any specific ethnic demographic. There is also a growing number of Black and Brown "none" and "de-churched" young men and women. The Jude 3 Project and the Black Millennial Café, in partnership with the Barna Group, are beginning to bring attention to this reality. This is important because the ever-increasing multiethnic emerging generations are truly a wake-up call for the entire body of Christ in the United States.

FOR YOUR CONSIDERATION

Church Leader: How has your church sought to maintain connection with young adults heading off to college and encouraged them to experience Christian community there and on their periodic returns home?

Sitting in the Pew: What stories have you heard from young people experiencing life in a new setting? How are you helping them feel heard?

Millennial/Gen Z: What has kept you connected to a faith community even while experiencing the world differently from when you were younger?

All In: This book goes far beyond encouraging ethnic diversity in a church. In what ways does your church reflect the surrounding neighborhood and in what ways does it not?

1

EMERGING GENERATIONS
AND THE CHURCH

THE NUMERICAL DECLINE of the church in the United States has come rather suddenly and contrasts significantly with its timeline in other Western nations. Certainly, Covid-19 has had a long-term impact on worship habits and involvement that is still being understood, but overall, church involvement remains comparatively high compared to other nations.

Only the United States saw an upsurge in both attendance and influence of the church throughout the middle of the twentieth century. Attendance levels were relatively stable through the 1960s at approximately 40 percent of the general population, significantly higher than many other parts of the Western world.[1] However, since that time the decline has been precipitous. While the Fuller Youth Institute suggests that the greatest decrease in numbers is being experienced in traditional mainline denominations such as Presbyterian, Lutheran, Episcopal, Methodist, and American Baptist, the phenomenon is being witnessed in churches everywhere.[2]

Long gone are the days immediately following World War II, when the church was at its zenith in terms of strength and cultural influence in a society that found meaning in institutional belonging.[3] These shared communities of belief brought with them an impression of unity, either real or imagined, and the assumption that the nation was culturally unified. However, this is no longer the case. As Dwight Zscheile points out:

Transcendent cultural frameworks for meaning in American society have eroded, and nothing has arisen to replace them. Underneath there is a deeper shift in late modernity toward the individual self being the ultimate source of authority. Established structures and roles that once provided identity, meaning, and community have been supplanted by an expressive individualism that seeks out liberation from structure and tradition through endless choice.[4]

This is the world in which emerging generations find themselves. They are frequently caught in the dilemma of having to secure meaning and purpose for themselves outside of the institutions that provided these in generations past.[5] While they still desire to discern their own sense of meaning and purpose, many no longer perceive the church as an institution in which they can find answers to their deep questions. This difficulty becomes clear when considering the widening age gap regarding religious affiliation. In the same Pew Research study cited previously, three-quarters of baby boomers described themselves as Christian, while only 49 percent of those in the millennial generation claimed the same.[6]

Those criticizing the disconnect of the church with the changing social landscape have not been limited to those outside the church.[7] Although some find comfort in the apparent growth of several notable megachurches, overall attendance continues to fall relative to population.[8] The attrition rate of churches is most pronounced in those born after 1980; this group has gained several monikers, but as a whole are described as the emerging generations. They currently represent approximately 23 percent of the US population; however, the Faith Communities Today research team has determined that only about one in ten Christian congregations see anything close to that percentage attending on any regular basis.[9]

The effects of this are evident throughout the United States, and not limited to specific regions of the country; it includes the so-called Bible Belt. Though it may be difficult to comprehend, statistically speaking, according to author John Seel, "another American church shutters its doors every 2.5 hours. Churches thrive for a number of reasons, but they close for one reason—a failure to reach the next generation."[10]

Some in evangelical traditions find comfort when comparing themselves to mainline churches, which are experiencing a much greater and often faster decline. Yet even the largest denomination in the country, the Southern Baptist Convention, reported earlier this year that it was currently experiencing its twelfth year of declining membership.[11] Those denominations that many consider the healthiest are simply experiencing a less drastic rate of decline in comparison to others. Individual congregations that appear to be bucking the trend of decline may only be doing so through consolidating individuals from smaller congregations, as they transfer to larger and more vibrant branches of Christian community. Author Paula McGee disparagingly refers to this as the "Walmartization" of the church.[12]

According to several research sources there is absolutely no evident growth nationwide through new professions of faith.[13] This could be the result of either rejection of all institutional belonging, or a new way of belonging for those in emerging generations that is more organic and less structured. The pandemic that disrupted all aspects of life has only exacerbated this reality, and for many broke them of any habit of church attendance they might have maintained.

However, most observers studying the trends find one statistic increasingly disconcerting. Pew Research indicates that, in addition to the numerical decline, the influence of Christianity continues to wane.[14] This is in large part due to the demographic categories of people who are represented in the decline. Over the last decade or so, the numbers of the religiously unaffiliated and unattached have risen to a point almost equal with those described as evangelicals, and are apparently growing at a faster rate than any other religious segment, from 9 percent in 1993 to 29 percent in 2019.[15]

Even more alarming for some is that this growing religiously unaffiliated group is particularly strong among emerging generations.[16] Kimberly Winston suggests that the nones "claim either no religious preference or no religion at all."[17] They are a religiously unattached, unaffiliated group of individuals, including those who self-describe as atheist, agnostic, and "nothing in particular." Although they are not at all uniform in many other respects, they are becoming an increasingly important demographic in several areas, shaping economic and social dynamics in new and unforeseen ways.[18] John Seel reports that they strongly prefer experiential learning, "where embodiment takes precedence over cognition, practice over principle, street over book smarts, and lived experience over classroom theory."[19] Thus, they almost universally prefer story and experience over worldview and theology.[20]

Such an erosion of faith adherents causes many to fear that before long, numerical decline may bring many faith-based businesses, academic institutions, and denominations into even greater financial strife and further denigrate the influence of the church on national and world affairs. There is a clear generational gap in religious ideologies between those born prior to 1980 and those born after. "Religiously unaffiliated Americans are significantly younger than religiously affiliated Americans, with more than one-third coming from those under the age of thirty."[21] Thus, not only is the church not growing, it continues to age, with a significant portion of the ongoing numerical decline caused by the deaths of those from older generations.

To gain some understanding of the underlying beliefs of many in emerging generations, particularly those self-described as "nones," one might look to what has become, for many, one of their defining annual cultural events. The Burning Man community event, first held in the 1980s, is one window into the values and thinking of many young people.[22] Seel suggests that this movement provides much needed insight into the developing attitudes of this generation. The movement is based on ten key principles:

1. No Boundaries/Radical Inclusion
2. Gifting
3. Decommodification
4. Radical Self-Reliance
5. Radical Self-Expression
6. Communal Effort
7. Civic Responsibility
8. Leaving No Trace
9. Participation
10. Immediacy[23]

While these do not appear to be blatantly antagonistic to the Christian faith, there is a sense that festival participants believe these values are not to be found in religion or traditional faith communities. There seems to be an understanding among the Burning Man adherents that individuals are to be accepted and respected as they are—which for many has not been their experience in the traditional church.

However, one should not presume, based on their withdrawal from traditional religious communities, that those in emerging generations are overtly antagonistic to faith practices, religious beliefs, or spirituality. Although the work of the Fuller Youth Institute might suggest that many are disenchanted with church and religion, youth have not completely broken these connections.[24] They appear to adhere to many traditional Judeo-Christian beliefs, while at the same time preferring to experience their faith independently and through personal introspection, often disconnected from organized religious institutions.[25] This apparent lack of hostility toward religion highlights another concerning trend: it seems that the absence of hostility and antagonism is likely a result of their general apathy toward organized religion and its institutions. They just don't care about it all that much.[26]

Even for those who have had some form of ongoing connection with the church, it seems that few have gained much in their religious upbringing that is durable enough to sustain them once they graduate out of organized youth programs.[27] Even if we believe that the disconnect of emerging generations is only temporary, hoping that many of them will return to the fold of institutional faith once they settle down and begin to have families of their own, there remain concerns. As the Fuller Youth Institute points out in describing the reasons behind their research for the book *Growing Young*, "even those who return will have made significant life decisions about worldview, relationships, and vocation—all during an era when their faith was shoved aside."[28] It is difficult to fathom the long-term implications of this possibility, but more than likely, it will mean that church involvement will remain secondary to those other life contexts unless a substantial spiritual transformation occurs within their lives.

This disconnect raises critical future management questions for traditional church institutions as most are dependent on the consistent personal involvement of people for tithing, volunteer work, and community interaction. Continued withdrawal of emerging generations will mandate an alteration of current structures for these institutions to survive. The church and other Christian institutions have managed to endure because of the high levels of involvement of more connected generations. Traditionally the church measured its health based on the "ABCs"—attendance, buildings, and cash.[29] These are no longer sufficient measures to understand the genuine health of the church. However, sadly, economic rather than spiritual concerns are likely to drive efforts to reengage with emerging generations.[30]

POSTMODERNISM AND THE TECHNOLOGICAL AGE

Much has also been written in recent years about postmodernism and its impact on young adults. Changes in thinking, convictions, values, family structure, and modes of learning have all altered the way young people perceive and engage with their surroundings.[31] Society continues in a period of transition from modernism to postmodernism, which means that there is often an ideological divide between emerging generations and older adults in terms of the way they experience and understand the world.

The financial resources in the United States were greater and more broadly available after World War II than at any earlier period in the history of the nation. This instigated the drive for upward mobility and financial independence, a greater willingness to make geographical moves for career development, and thus the growth of the nuclear family. The familial isolation, brought about by normalizing the nuclear family model, encouraged a change in values that had been relatively stable for generations, thus highlighting an emphasis on "individualism, personal freedom as self-fulfillment, and greater tolerance of diversity."[32] While postmodernism is not a direct result of these lifestyle choices, taken together, they did encourage a measurable shift in values that has had a significant impact on traditional Christian faith communities and institutions. These shifts have only been exacerbated recently with the global pandemic, the heightened racial tensions, and the increased political polarization since the spring of 2020.

The impact of postmodernism is felt throughout Western society but appears to cause particular concern regarding religious faith experience and expression. Many researchers have argued that there is an ideological conflict between the modernist perspective coming out of the Enlightenment, which is the basis of much Western religious thought, and the postmodernist thought patterns of emerging adults. The effect of postmodernism, with its inherent skepticism, subjectivism, and relativism, is confusing and frustrating to emerging generations. It raises deep questions about the value of involvement in a traditional Christian faith community.[33] Assumptions made by previous generations regarding the value of religious life and its importance to understanding the world in which we live are no longer accepted implicitly. As a result, many young people leave the faith community, which they no longer feel is in balance with other aspects of their lives.

Others have suggested that there are too many competing stresses in life, preventing the deep immersion in religious life that is necessary to derive any meaningful connection within and value from church involvement. Rampant consumerism, which is a key cultural value in the Western world, particularly the United States, impacts one's freedom to participate in things that do not easily generate immediate economic value and security. The spiritual disconnect may also simply be a result of too many other interesting options vying for a finite amount of time. Involvement in a Christian faith community may be one of those options that is most readily dismissed as a result.

In addition to the changes taking place regarding thought processes within the wider society, a largely unanticipated transformation has occurred impacting almost every aspect of life. The technological age provides the ability to be constantly connected digitally to music and entertainment, online retail sites, as well as social media platforms that have a worldwide influence. This capacity has altered much about the way people experience the world, and the Covid-19 pandemic has only increased this influence and even moved many aspects of church life onto a digital platform.[34] Young people have never known life without these technologies.

The ability to link with people all over the world has arguably caused a greater willingness to accept diversity and tolerance of diversity. There have also been some concerning drawbacks to the present hyperconnectivity. As research continues into the effects this is having, it seems that one of the most significant changes is that society is now "a world of constant digital interruption, continuously fragmented attention, and multitasking. The result is an erosion of people's capacity to be present to one another or hold face-to-face conversations," particularly with those of differing ideas.[35] This creates yet another challenge to faith congregations founded on meaningful community engagement and interaction. Miroslav Volf argues:

> In cultures shaped by modernity, we have come to live "disembedded" lives. No longer experiencing ourselves as constituents of a meaningful cosmos and members of a social body, we modern human beings imagine ourselves and act first and foremost as individuals, ideally sovereign owners of ourselves and our actions.[36]

The demise of meaningful community may be one of the consequences of the inundation of technology in contemporary life. The hope within the church community is that it may also be a catalyst for encouraging young people back into dynamic and diverse faith communities.

The isolation that separates people from experiencing true community even has the potential to further limit crosscultural interaction. Much research continues to be conducted on the impact of the ubiquitous nature of the internet and social media connection. One apparent repercussion has been heightened cultural polarization. Zscheile comments,

> Digital media allows people to choose from an endless array of cultural channels. The result is a new micro-tribalism. . . .

It fosters cultural segregation and the collapse of common spaces and narratives. Assumptions are often reinforced rather than challenged, and it is easy to demonize those with whom we disagree.[37]

So, the paradox of contemporary life seems to be greater cultural diversity with concurrent heightened isolation and division resulting from maintaining narrow digital interaction. Unfortunately, the church is struggling with similar issues, which limits any opportunity it might have of providing a positive example and influence.

As someone who has been in youth ministry for most of my adult life, I am constantly amazed at the impact technology has on all of us, particularly how it has changed the way young people connect with each other and their faith. At several recent youth events, I witnessed young people responding to challenging messages from speakers or difficult discussions in small groups by reaching for their phones as soon as they could to connect with their "tribe" and share their discomfort. This did not allow time for processing or discussing with leaders in order to seek understanding and grow in knowledge and deepen their faith. It led to concerned calls from parents during the retreats, worried about their child, and resulted in additional stress and work for the youth staff—who were now distracted from ministering to the students in their group by simply working to ensure that no one got offended. It made me very thankful that the bulk of my time in youth ministry was prior to the cell phone age. It also confirmed to me how technology provides chances to broaden engagement with a diverse world but allows isolation to continue at the same time.

These social changes are certainly influencing the relationship between emerging generations and the church. However, to place the blame for empty pews on these seemingly uncontrollable external forces is too simple, and fails to address other factors for which the church is more overtly responsible.[38] The ongoing segregated nature of the church in the United States is one significant concern that has yet to be addressed adequately. It is believed that transforming congregations into communities that are more reflective of their surrounding demographics will address some aspects of church involvement that are most uninviting to emerging generations.

THE MONOCULTURAL NATURE OF THE CHURCH

The authors of *Neighborhood Church* suggest that, when traditional Christian communities lack the diversity experienced by emerging generations in almost every other aspect of their lives, this exacerbates the sense that the church is failing to capture "the imagination, authenticity and risk-willingness of this generation."[39] It's that limited diversity that this book is most concerned with. As societies around the world continue to transform—ethnically, culturally, and socially—the seeming inability for much of the church to reflect these alterations may be providing yet another reason for emerging generations to disengage. If nothing else, as Efrem suggests in a previous book, the monocultural nature of the church at least gives them an additional excuse for disconnecting.[40]

One of the significant challenges for the church in the Western world is that it remains almost universally segregated. To emerging generations, this often communicates that it is an institution trapped in the past. There are likely several reasons for the continued segregation, but it seems that implicit bias is at the core of the issue. Even with the growth of the multiethnic church movement, now representing upward of 16 percent of churches, the overall culture and theology within may continue to be largely monocultural.[41] Therefore, because of these issues, the institutional church may be tacitly communicating a sense of bigotry, racism, and exclusivity, all of which are the antithesis of what should be perceived.

In general, when people consider the "average" church in the United States, their ideas center around images of middle-class White people gathered together on a Sunday morning. Without a doubt, the church influence in the United States continues to remain in the control of a largely monocultural White middle-class mindset. James Hunter argues, "In the early decades of the twenty-first century as in the last decades of the twentieth, Christian presence in America has been a presence primarily in, of, and for the middle class in everything that this designation means."[42]

For the vast majority of those born after 1980, this monoculturalism is not indicative of almost any other aspect of their lives, including education, career, social organizations, and neighborhood. The level of discomfort they feel in contexts bereft of diversity appears to impact their perception of those monocultural institutions.

The surge of diversity, ethnic and otherwise, is also increasing rapidly. Pew Research determined that those born after 1997 will be the most diverse generation ever seen in the United States.[43] Within emerging generations, the statistics might be somewhat surprising. For the youngest of these, born between 1997 and 2011, only a small majority of them, 52 percent, are non-Hispanic White; it is anticipated that those born from 2012 onward will become the first generation lacking any ethnic majority.[44] Further, many of these young people have a multicultural heritage of their own. Terry Linhart draws on additional Pew Research to say, "Twenty-five percent of those who are under eighteen years of age in the United States live with at least one parent who is an immigrant."[45]

Paul Sorrentino, author and leader of a multiethnic campus ministry, writes, "People in their twenties and teens have grown up in a society that values multi-culturalism. They are used to diverse classroom settings and sports teams. It is what they expect. When they do not see it in the church, they are disillusioned."[46] Not only does this disillusionment cause them to question aspects of their faith experience, it also strongly communicates to them that the church intentionally maintains divisions, excluding those perceived as others. To them, this division is hypocritical and contrary to what the church overtly espouses. Organizations that either resist efforts

toward diversity or struggle to become more diverse in both participants and leadership will likely continue falling out of favor with
emerging generations.

The Christian church must reflect an inclusive rather than an
exclusive body of believers, as described in the book of Acts. There
must be intentional efforts to enhance diversity that provide opportunity for people from all walks of life to not only participate
passively, but to share responsibility for leadership, decision making,
and discipleship in a manner that encourages engagement from
multiple perspectives.

Young people are more comfortable in diverse environments, as
this is generally more reflective of all other aspects of their lives.
Thus, as they move from their home environs due to education or
work, they are potentially less likely to seek out a faith community
that lacks much in the way of diversity, ethnic or otherwise. If, in
fact, they do desire connection with a Christian faith community,
what they are seeking is equivalent to other aspects of their daily
lives. According to this insight, one of the reasons many in emerging
generations are moving away from Christian faith communities is
that these faith communities appear to remain stuck in earlier ways
of living in the world, ones that offer little meaningful interaction
with those who look and think differently than themselves.

Now, the lack of diversity within the church is understandable.
Faith is often very personal, central to the way in which the world
is interpreted and understood. Kenny Walden argues that especially
in such personal issues as belief and faith, "people have an inclination to seek out those who mirror their own thoughts, actions
and images."[47] While some churches are trying to be more inclusive
and foster diversity in their faith communities, most are finding
this a particular challenge; they remain overwhelmingly monocultural in all but a few localized instances.[48] Certainly, this lack of
diversity is not limited to older, more traditional, mainline denominations. It is an issue throughout the Western world. However, for

these mainline denominations it is certainly something that needs to be recognized as a potential contributing factor to their aging and shrinking membership.

OTHER CULTURAL CHANGES

Western culture has impacted young people and Christian faith communities in other, less overt ways as well. This is particularly true regarding the rampant consumerism that is evident in every corner of society. This ideology has infected all aspects of life, even personal spirituality. Consumeristic tendencies develop at an early age and impact perception of the world in more than simply material goods.[49] They affect pursuit of all forms of fulfillment and satisfaction. The belief is that if a need is recognized, there is a simple solution that the consumption of a product or ideology will satisfy. This is evident in church life and is demonstrated by the phenomenon that most church growth occurs as a result of transfer rather than profession of faith.[50] The assumption is that movement to a new faith community will satiate a need that was unmet previously.

People tend to "shop" for a church that caters to their needs of the moment. When those needs are no longer met or new needs appear that can be better satisfied elsewhere, the shopping recommences. Though it is certainly not limited to younger generations, this shopping does seem to impact them at greater levels as they demonstrate less allegiance to denominational structure. Even more disheartening is the idea that one can satiate spiritual needs through correct application of consumeristic efforts. Soong-Chan Rah laments the fact that "spiritual life becomes a consumable product that is exchanged only if it benefits the material and corporeal well-being of the individual consumer."[51] Without a sense that clear and overt benefits derive from maintaining involvement with a faith community, it seems that emerging generations are exploring other options to satiate some of their internal needs.

Even those who maintain an affiliation with a Christian community appear to do so with far less conviction than previous generations.[52] Christian Smith and Melissa Lundquist found in their national research of the religious habits of young people that, though a strong percentage of young people do maintain connection to faith communities, it seems that their ongoing involvement "simply does not mean that much or make much sense to many of them."[53] It is evident that many continue in faith practices out of habit or to maintain familial obligations, but have limited investment in these spiritual practices. Their involvement also appears to have limited influence on their lifestyle choices.

Kenda Creasy Dean, in her book *Almost Christian: What the Faith of Our Teenagers Is Telling the American Church*, argues that the inability of young people to articulate their faith hints at its shallowness. "Mainline Protestant young people are among the least religiously articulate of all teens, and Catholic youth follow close behind."[54] Yet this is not a concern solely of more traditional church contexts. The impact of the Covid-19 pandemic on the church of the future in altering the worship habits of individuals is not yet fully understood. Early evidence suggests that involvement remains down from previous years regardless of denominational affiliation. It is uncertain when or even if a rebound can be expected.

Doubt regarding the value and purpose of faith is evident in other ways as well. In a society that endorses the pursuit of one's dreams and promotes the idea that happiness is the main purpose of life, young people are encouraged to choose wisely from the lifestyle smorgasbord on offer. Religious communities are therefore simply one of a multitude of choices they have for finding fulfillment and direction. Yolanda Pantou writes, "For young people, the church and other established institutions, are one of many options, or are up for discussion. The existence of a variety of denominations is all the more reason for them to doubt the authority of the church."[55] The options available don't encourage commitment to things about which they are uncertain or undecided. Further, for young adults who do not understand denominational issues or distinctions, these details confirm separateness and division and do little to affirm a sense of unity or the value of involvement.

A SENSE OF PANIC

The statistical and societal changes discussed above tend to cause panic among church leaders as they fear the eventual collapse of the church and the resulting degradation of the moral fabric of society. Dan Kimball grimly predicts that "Christians are now foreigners in a post-Christian culture."[56] Where once societal expectations were sufficient to encourage consistent church involvement, this is no longer the case. Kenny Walden writes, "Churches can no longer rely solely on their tradition to automatically sustain increase or help bring meaning to their membership."[57] There are now too many other options for people to consider, ones that often require less sacrifice and fit more readily into a lifestyle that society endorses.

Although societal changes are evident, particularly in regard to emerging generations, Anthony Elliott believes the church is loath to believe how significant it is that "we live in new worlds of social and cultural organization."[58] Minor adjustments to church organization or structure will have negligible impact on engaging the disaffected. It is a new world altogether and requires a completely new approach as a result. While this does not mean that all tradition should be discarded, it does suggest that, if the church is to remain at all central to the morals and cultural values in the future, it must embrace a theology that engages with emerging generations, fully reflecting the inclusiveness found in the message of the gospel. The church can no longer isolate itself from culture to maintain some semblance of purity. William Dyrness realizes that this has never been truer: "There is no way for the church to interact constructively with contemporary culture without being rooted firmly both in that culture and in the biblical and Christian tradition."[59]

IS THERE ANY HOPE?

The narrative of unremitting church decline is not the full story. While a decrease in church attendance is certainly happening, there is strong evidence to suggest that less monochromatic faith communities remain vibrant and may even be growing. Soong-Chan Rah, author of *The Next Evangelicalism*, describes "the reality of twenty-first century American Christianity—the White churches are in decline while the immigrant, ethnic and multiethnic churches are flourishing."[60] This more optimistic view provides some hope for the church of the future, but again, there remain concerns resulting from the ongoing changes brought about by the pandemic.

So it's important to consider the church more broadly than simply the suburban, middle-class, monocultural version to fully grasp its connection within emerging generations. According to Rah the problem lies in the fact that the usual focus of concern is the accepted "normal" American church, White and middle class. He says, "As many lament the decline of Christianity in the United States in the twenty-first century, very few have recognized that American Christianity may actually be growing, but in unexpected and surprising ways."[61] While this statement contradicts the research of the Fuller Youth Institute that there is no observable growth, it does make the case that inherent assumptions about what the church is may influence the interpretation of what is occurring and even impact how research is conducted and discerned.

DISCERNING THE WAY FORWARD

In the age of social media, when it appears that relationships have become superficial, it seems that genuine connection and acceptance in a vibrant faith community would be attractive and inviting. Donald Lewis and Richard Pierard are convinced that "the central idea is that the world is becoming more and more a single place, a single 'village,' with all the outcomes this has on human relations and the way we see the world."[62] This single "village" is far more diverse than in previous generations and should be reflected within all the most important institutions, particularly the church.

What this means is that pursuing diversity or a church community that reflects the wider culture in terms of gender, ethnicity, age, and social strata needs to be more than just a gimmick or a short-term effort in order for the church to survive another few years. If diversity is the goal, it needs to be purposeful and have a foundation more profound than simply the latest ploy to attract and keep the next generation. It is far bigger and more important than responding to cultural changes. This is the church as God intended. These developments may line up with what is occurring in emerging generations, but they should occur because we are responding to what the church is designed to reflect: God's love for the whole of humanity.

This book will develop the idea that several factors foster the ongoing engagement of emerging generations. They desire a strong sense of inclusion and belonging in a community that acts as an extended family network, expressing genuine care and concern for them as they are. They expect that they will be permitted to participate fully in the life of the congregation, not simply because they show up at times of corporate worship, but because they have something tangible and meaningful to offer. They also expect that worship and messages connect to their everyday lives.[63] Though these things can happen in a monocultural congregational environment, the work that is necessary to foster genuine diversity within a worship community will strengthen these qualities and garner stronger connection and deeper commitment from the young people less inclined to be there.

Ultimately, this is our underlying motivation for writing this book. It represents an attempt to encourage the church to become more representative of the community God desires and reflective of the local neighborhood surrounding congregations. Investigations into the changes occurring within emerging generations highlight their increasing diversity. Therefore, it seems prudent to discern any link between emerging generations and diversity in the church.

Chapter two of this book presents how the church as God desires it to exist is the ideal place where the needs of young people can be expressed and ultimately find fulfillment within that community. Chapter three provides examples of congregations that have embraced a multi-inclusive ethic, providing a context for young people to become actively involved in transforming their world with the gospel. Chapter four addresses some of the challenges experienced by churches attempting to embrace a multi-inclusive ethic. It reminds us that working toward this goal is not a marketing gimmick, but a transformational change in the nature and makeup of the entire church. Chapter five recognizes that each generation has a desire to positively impact the world in which they live. It develops the idea that the multi-inclusive church is the perfect context to harness the specific passions of emerging generations as means of living out the gospel. Chapter six explains that the divisions found in the church are not limited to ethnicity; it explains the history behind the exclusivity and why it remains so difficult to shift Christian culture toward a more inclusive expression. Chapter seven develops the biblical foundations for the multi-inclusive church, providing evidence from both the Old and New Testaments that this was God's plan from the beginning. Finally, chapter eight provides multiple examples of churches growing in diversity, demonstrating that there are multiple ways to approach the challenge of becoming multi-inclusive. It will also include suggestions for helping current church members embrace the need to become more inclusive so that all feel welcome in their faith community.

The segregated and monocultural church is an issue that continues to have repercussions throughout the world regardless of denomination or geographic location. Our hope is that this book will not be limited to a specific denomination or locality, but that it will raise questions and help guide the thinking of all those who desire to engender a more complete reflection of the community of God.

FOR YOUR CONSIDERATION

Church Leader: How effectively do you feel your congregation has been in meeting the needs of those in emerging generations described here? How reflective of your surrounding community is your congregation, and what message might that be sending to those outside your church?

Sitting in the Pew: How comfortable are you with any change that might be necessary to make your church more inviting and inclusive? What role do you think you have in helping make that happen?

Millennial/Gen Z: What are the stories behind those you know who view the church with side eyes? What is it about your faith community that has kept you connected? How can this be replicated for others?

All In: Have any of the issues mentioned here impacted you personally? How has the church been a safe and healthy place for you to work through them? What have been some of the challenges associated with these issues and your congregational home?

2

ADDRESSING EMERGING
GENERATIONS THROUGH
THE MULTI-INCLUSIVE CHURCH

PASTOR DAN KIMBALL, senior pastor of Vintage Faith Church in Santa Cruz, California, wrote a book in 2007 called *They Like Jesus but Not the Church: Insights from Emerging Generations*. His premise was that though emerging generations were increasingly struggling with the church, especially the evangelical church, they still had a relatively positive view of Jesus. If this is still the case, is there an opportunity for the church to reach emerging generations by focusing on shared aspects of our common faith, those things that highlight our unity as disciples of Jesus, rather than our doctrinal and denominational divisions?

Though we want to believe that the focus of the Western church is on Jesus Christ, this is not always the perspective of those outside the church. For some, the church seems to be about pastors, buildings, money, growth, and power. Social media is full of accounts building up the brand of pastors. We authors, as men with accounts on every social media platform, must begin by looking at ourselves and asking, "How am I using this tool, and who am I ultimately pointing people to?"

Am I just trying to become the next celebrity pastor? And beyond my own power, is the church just about buildings? As I (Efrem) write this chapter, my church is in a building campaign. Is the building the focus? Our church must wrestle with how the mission of Christ is accomplished in a real way through a building. Money and growth aren't categorically bad things. We see the Christian community growing in the New Testament, even amid significant persecution. We see generosity thanks to the financial resources that come from selling property.

The question is, are the people and the resources of the church pointing to the declarations and demonstrations of Christ? We believe that this is ultimately what emerging generations are searching for and need. David T. Olsen, in his book *The American Church in Crisis*, argues that the message of Jesus must be re-centered in the church. This lack of authentic centering of Christ could be the main reason the church is in decline in the United States. Christ is the embodiment of the good news. Olson reminds us that this good news includes compassion and justice.

Jesus interacted with people in a respectful and attentive manner. People were not a means to an end, but themselves had intrinsic value. "He causes his sun to rise on the evil and the good, and sends rain on the righteous and the unrighteous" (Matthew 5:45). The theological basis for this saying rested on twin teachings from the Torah. First, Yahweh is revealed as a God who is righteous, is full of compassion, and demands justice. Second, he also is Creator, who made all humans in his image. Jesus showed this heart of mercy in how he loved people, particularly the poor, the sick, and the marginalized.[1]

When Christ walked the earth in human form, he called people to follow him. His following was both intergenerational and multiethnic. Men, women, children, the poor, the outcast, the privileged, and the incarcerated were drawn to him. Christ must ultimately be the draw of the emerging generations to the church. Christ is the center of the inclusive, multiethnic, and reconciling church. Christ spoke of the kingdom of God—but Christ also *demonstrated* the kingdom of God. Put another way, he presented what it looks like when the kingdom of God invades a broken world.

Christ had a kingdom agenda beyond those who saw themselves as the chosen people of God. His kingdom agenda included Samaritan women, tax collectors, lepers, those facing the death penalty, and a multitude of others excluded by religious authorities from full participation. His kingdom agenda was multiethnic, multicultural, and multi-inclusive. This is because the means of separation are transcended in the kingdom of God.

The multiethnic, multi-inclusive, and reconciling church should serve as a picture of the multiethnic and multicultural kingdom of God and embody the complete agenda of Christ. The problem is that a segment of evangelicalism seems opposed to multiculturalism and a justice-oriented vision of the gospel. The word *justice* in parts of evangelicalism is seen as socialist ideology, or even Marxist, and antithetical to Scripture. This is very ironic considering how many times the word *justice* is found in Scripture.

Evangelicalism has been slow in prioritizing multiethnic church planting over homogeneous models of church planting. And, in many cases, the multiethnic church planting and revitalization models are based on assimilating into White cultural ministry expressions. Christian sociologist Korie Edwards provides an example of this kind of assimilation in her book *The Elusive Dream*, where she studies a multiethnic church called Crosstown: "Relative to other conservative Protestant African Americans, African Americans at Crosstown demonstrated greater susceptibility to the dominant white (particularly white evangelical) ideology about racial inequality in the United States."[2]

So what should shape the DNA of these multiethnic, inclusive, and justice-oriented churches? They should be rooted in a vision of the kingdom of God coming to bear in the diversity and division within the mission field now found throughout much of the developed world, and embody the mission of Christ. Therefore, a practical theology of the incarnation of Christ is vital. These churches must emphasize Christ as Reconciler, Savior, Messiah, and Liberator. Christ is the best example of the nature and character of God. In Scripture, Christ brings good news to the sinner, the diseased, the paralyzed, and the left-for-dead. He does this crossculturally and intergenerationally. Talk about a movement of diversity and inclusion! This authentic Christ of the Scriptures is needed like never before in a mission field that is both increasingly multiethnic and deeply divided. The church has lost its way by being known more for its allegiance to race, nation, and political ideology than the revolutionary good news of Christ. We need a rediscovery, or a genuine first-time discovery, of a church that embodies the good news of Christ in this full sense: a true discovery of the incarnation.

The incarnation of God through the declarations and demonstrations of Christ is testament to God as the ultimate reconciler and the head of the multi-inclusive church. As the greatest revelation of God's love, Christ reconciles sinful humanity to God and divided humanity to one another. This chapter explores how God's empowering and transformative love informs the church. It also unpacks how an understanding of Christ as one who came to earth as the marginalized Messiah and Liberator of the oppressed empowers members of the church to mirror the inclusiveness of God in Christ. Finally, we will offer a reconciliation theology that shows the missional intersection of crosscultural disciple making, reconciliation praxis, and justice.

THE INCARNATION
AND RECONCILIATION MINISTRY PRAXIS

God is love—it's a theme that runs throughout all of Scripture. The greatest expression of God's love for humanity is found within the incarnation of God in Christ. God as love is revealed in the reconciling work of Christ. In *The Message*, Eugene Peterson translates the first chapter of John as follows:

The Word became flesh and blood,
    and moved into the neighborhood.
We saw the glory with our own eyes,
    the one-of-a-kind glory,
    like Father, like Son,
Generous inside and out,
    true from start to finish. (John 1:14 MSG)

The suggestion that the Son of God "moved into the neighborhood" speaks powerfully that Jesus was the one doing the accommodating. This might come as a surprise to emerging generations, who tend to assume that the church expects engagement on its own terms, thus communicating exclusivity. Jesus accommodated himself to the culture and experiences of those being served, thus demonstrating a vibrant inclusivity.

The extent of God's love for broken and divided humanity is demonstrated by Jesus' direct social proximity to humanity. God goes beyond a supernatural voice to Adam and Eve, a burning bush to Moses, or sending angels as representatives. God becomes human in Christ Jesus. The all-holy, all-powerful, and only true God came into the world as flesh in Christ. This is what makes the incarnation not only the foundation of reconciliation, but radical. It introduces a whole new understanding of God. God is not simply a distant God who can only be known in supernatural, cosmic expressions. God can also be known in the natural form of a human being, with the purpose of salvation, liberation, and justice. Theologian James H. Cone explains the incarnation of God in the following manner:

> The grounding of liberation in God's act in Jesus Christ is the logical consequence of any Christian theology that takes Scripture seriously as an important source for the doing of theology. . . . It also expresses God's will to be in relation to creatures in the social context of their striving for the fulfillment of humanity. That is, God is free to be for us. This is

the meaning of the Exodus and the Incarnation. . . . God is the God of Jesus Christ who calls the helpless and weak into a newly created existence.[3]

This is what potentially connects so powerfully with emerging generations. It re-creates community that fosters inclusivity rather than the exclusivity that seemed more prevalent within the Pharisee classes in the time of Jesus. Christ becomes one of us so that all of us who make up the human family have access to liberation and reconciliation. God becomes human and enters the social divides of male and female, privileged and marginalized, colonizer and exiled, as well as those deemed righteous and those excluded. Christ is born in an underresourced setting among farm animals. Under the government-sanctioned threat of Hebrew male babies being annihilated, Christ and his earthly parents flee into Egypt as immigrants. Christ is beaten unmercifully by a military-police-like force of the Roman Empire. Christ is wrongfully arrested and receives the death penalty, though the governing authorities admit finding no fault in him.

These experiences of God revealed in Christ show that God does not simply *have* compassion and mercy for the immigrant, the incarcerated, the poor, and the marginalized. God in Christ *became* the immigrant, the incarcerated, the poor, and the marginalized. Theologian Howard Thurman addresses the relevance of the context and ethnicity in which God shows up as human:

> It is necessary to examine the religion of Jesus against the background of his own age and people, and to inquire into the content of his teaching with reference to the disinherited and the underprivileged. We begin with the simple historical fact that Jesus was a Jew. The miracle of the Jewish people is almost as breathtaking as the miracle of Jesus. . . . The economic predicament with which he was identified in birth placed him initially with the great mass of men on earth. The masses of

the people are poor. If we dare take the position that in Jesus there was at work some radical destiny, it would be safe to say that in his poverty he was more truly Son of man than he would have been if the incident of family or birth had made him a rich son of Israel.[4]

Thurman sheds light on how spiritually and socially radical the incarnation of God is. The radicality is found in that Jesus doesn't simply attempt to include the marginalized but became one of them when taking human form. This informs the ministry praxis of the church because it reveals how God chooses to be reconciled to sinful humanity, ensuring none will be excluded because they are found on the margins of society. This also provides the opportunity for humanity to experience reconciliation in a way that deals with the various social divisions systemically and relationally between human beings. God addresses the social divisions within humanity by entering those divisions as a human being. Reconciliation theologian John Perkins highlights the social impact of the incarnation of God:

> God was able to identify with us because He came down from heaven to be a man. He relocated. You don't get to the heart of people faster than when you go live with them and eat with them and fellowship with them—that gets you to peoples' hearts faster than anything else.[5]

Genuinely living in this same manner as disciples of Jesus breaks down the walls of resistance built up against the church because of perceived judgmentalism.

This deep connection of the incarnation of God with the marginalized and oppressed informs the identity of crosscultural and justice-oriented disciple makers within the church. Members of the church who are pursuing intentional reconciliation and genuine relationship go beyond compassion for the marginalized and oppressed to finding community and extended family with them.

Justice ministry in this light is communal both with the one in need of justice and with God. God calls the reconciling church into the same solidarity with the marginalized and oppressed that God also participates in through the incarnation.

The incarnation of God revealed in Christ is both a reconciliation between God and humanity and between divided humanity itself. This work of Christ provides salvific reconciliation, and it models social reconciliation. The ministry praxis of the church should embody both the vertical and horizontal dimensions of reconciliation and restoration. Failure to do so only limits the transformation and inclusive community that should be the result of the gospel.

In this way, the incarnation of God offers a missional ecclesiology for the church. God shows complete love for humanity, despite our sin, through the incarnation. God's love prioritizes social proximity and inclusivity. God in the human form of Christ gets up close to the diseased, the left-for-dead, the blind, the paralyzed, and the outcast. That is what the incarnation is; it is God being proximate. This is God being visibly intimate with humanity in all its expressions. The implication is that the church must be proximate to the oppressed, suffering, and excluded. While certainly Christ identifies most closely with the oppressed and suffering, his salvific love was also inclusive of the religious leaders. He called them to both view those around them as the Father does and to join with him in bringing about the full manifestation of the reign of God.

The ministry of the apostle Paul represents one example of how the incarnation of God in Christ and its reconciling and restorative work can be embraced and embodied in the transformation of the church. In his second letter to the church in the city of Corinth, Paul provides a missional ecclesiology connecting the love of God, the incarnation of God in Christ, a communal praxis, and the message and ministry of reconciliation and restoration as the mission of the church. He presents this missional ecclesiology:

For Christ's love compels us, because we are convinced that one died for all, and therefore all died. And he died for all, that those who live should no longer live for themselves but for him who died for them and was raised again. So from now on we regard no one from a worldly point of view. Though we once regarded Christ in this way, we do so no longer. Therefore, if anyone is in Christ, the new creation has come: The old has gone, the new is here! All this is from God, who reconciled us to himself through Christ and gave us the ministry of reconciliation: that God was reconciling the world to himself in Christ, not counting people's sins against them. And he has committed to us the message of reconciliation. (2 Corinthians 5:14-19)

These words of the apostle Paul offer an opportunity for the church to rediscover the incarnation by missionally living it out in the present within its local contexts. The mission of God revealed in Christ goes beyond simply being individually saved from sin through the reconciling work of Christ. We are spiritually saved by God's love revealed in Christ, but we are also spiritually empowered and socially transformed by it as well. Christ forgives sins, but also causes the lame to walk and gives sight to the blind. God's incarnational love found in Christ gives human beings access to eternal life and equips them in becoming ambassadors of reconciliation. Reconciliation and restoration come out of the overflow of God's love, brought close to sinful and divided humanity through Christ. This is the work of the church that has largely been missing, yet so powerfully resonates with the desire to be transformative evident in those in emerging generations.

EMBRACING AND EMBODYING THE INCARNATION

The people of the church in Corinth to whom Paul writes are oppressed and marginalized under the rule of the Roman Empire. Though the love of God is for all people, the incarnation of God in

Christ and the ecclesiastical mission of the apostle Paul are presented foremost to those under the empire's thumb. God's love is revealed to and received by the oppressed. It is from this reality that God loving the whole world cannot be refuted. God's love being revealed to the oppressed and marginalized strengthens the case that it is a love available to all. The incarnation of God brings reconciliation and salvation to sinful people and reconciliation and social transformation to divided people. This happens through God's empowering love, shown in the ministry activities of the church. Regarding how the church can embody the incarnation of God in this way, Cheryl Sanders writes,

> Whenever we feed the hungry, take in the homeless, visit the hospitals and nursing homes and prisons, we show God's promise to be true. We make good on the good news in the eyes of the dispossessed when we minister to them in the name of the Lord, because our ministry is God loving people through us—God feeds the poor in our kitchens, God comforts the lonely in our embrace, God heals the sick when we lay our hands on them, God consoles the prisoner with our words. This is the mandate of the kingdom, that the people of God cooperate with God by doing God's will.[6]

The church becomes a catalyst for reconciliation by embodying the love of God through ministries of solidarity with the marginalized, poor, and oppressed. The church must align its mission and purpose with the prophetic, redemptive, and justice-oriented ministry and mission of Christ.

This ministry of Christ meets a marginalized Samaritan woman at a well, it disrupts a woman caught in adultery from receiving the death penalty, it allows a touch from the hands of a woman with an incurable disease, and it speaks liberation to a terrorized man crying out from a cemetery. The multi-inclusive church must find its prophetic and justice-oriented place among the poor, marginalized, and oppressed in its surrounding community. Rather than identifying a niche demographic market to reach with our slick programs and engaging worship, congregations should be focused on all of those living within their surrounding communities, meeting their needs and demonstrating the acceptance and love of Christ in their midst.

The apostle John writes of the way God's love ought to compel us to find connection and community with all of those in our midst:

> This is how we know what love is: Jesus Christ laid down his life for us. And we ought to lay down our lives for our brothers and sisters. If anyone has material possessions and sees a brother or sister in need but has no pity on them, how can the love of God be in that person? Dear children, let us not love with words or speech but with actions and in truth. (1 John 3:16-18)

These words align well with Paul's including God's love in his reconciliation challenge to the church in Corinth. In stating that Christ's love compels us, Paul is pointing to God's love drawing in, controlling, and empowering human beings who embrace and embody the prophetic, reconciling, and justice-oriented ministry of Christ. Followers of Jesus are meant to be a people surrendered to and guided by God's empowering love revealed in Christ. Sinful human beings have shown from the beginning what they are able to do in their own power, separated from God's love. Human beings hate, discriminate, live in prejudice, use violence to solve conflict, sustain oppressive systems and institutions, and demonize others in their own power. But for human beings to sustain unity and justice, extend and receive forgiveness, and empower others, they need to receive and embody God's empowering and reconciling love revealed through the incarnation.

John Perkins is a champion of the type of theology and ministry praxis that embodies the incarnation of God. He is cofounder of the Christian Community Development Association (CCDA) and has ministered to the poor and oppressed in underresourced communities in California and Mississippi for over fifty years. Regarding how the church should embody the incarnation of God, Perkins states,

> Not only is the incarnation relocation; relocation is also incarnation. That is, not only did God relocate among us by taking the form of a man, but when a fellowship of believers relocates into a community, Christ invades that community. Christ, as His Body, as His church, comes to dwell there.[7]

Perkins demonstrates that the incarnation of God in Christ was not just a one-time act over two thousand years ago; through the church, it is the ongoing work of God. This is the challenge the apostle Paul put before the church in Corinth and is also the challenge that John Perkins is putting before the church today. The local church doesn't fulfill its purpose if it remains introspective and fails to be transformative within its surrounding community.

The reconciling church is one that has purposefully relocated where the marginalized, oppressed, and poor are. But just because a church is physically located in an underresourced community does not mean that its vision, mission, and ministry priorities represent a transformative focus on that community. The reconciling church is one that steps into the chasms of class, social, ethnic, gender, and racial divisions within its neighborhood community. The transformative church working to serve the needs of their entire community has the potential to be a bridge between movements such as Black Lives Matter and the police department or between families and community institutions that are failing them.

However, this creates challenges for the church that wants to transform their community. There are times when the church will need to stand on one side of the chasm where the poor, oppressed, and marginalized are, because of a failure of other institutions developed for that purpose. Jesus stood with the woman caught in adultery and faced the stone throwers who represented a corrupt criminal justice system on the other side of that social chasm. The church embodies Jesus when it stands with the poor, marginalized, and dispossessed, jointly facing the power structures that oppress them. These embodying activities move a multi-inclusive, multiethnic church beyond existing as a diverse congregation to missionally operating as a reconciling and transformative church community.

To be honest, Efrem's church in Sacramento seems far better placed to be a reconciling, transformative, multi-inclusive faith community than has been my experience in the churches I (Dan) have served. Some of that is a condition of location, but there is also great difficulty in moving a church that has been steeped in its own culture for generations. Planting a new congregation with diversity and inclusivity as one of its foundational cornerstones seems much less daunting to me. It often seems simpler to ride things out by maintaining the status quo.

My current congregation, outside of Atlanta, is trying to become just such a reconciling and transformative community—but it often feels like we are trying to make a U-turn with an oil tanker. Hiring diverse staff has been a start, allowing opportunities to get to know and better serve people in our immediate vicinity. These staff have helped us recognize some of the issues we did not understand and encouraged us to work with our neighbors in need, helping them face down some of the structures that seem determined to keep them down.

Recently, this has meant volunteers making appointments with the local mayor as the council was making moves to change an area designated as "workforce" housing, where many of the friends we seek to serve live. The council planned to tear this down for expensive townhouses that would strengthen the tax base within the city limits. Here we chose to stand on one side of the chasm, in solidarity with our friends and neighbors. Taking this stance was made more difficult because many of the council members and developers were known by those in our church.

The efforts are ongoing and, honestly, often discouraging. But hard and difficult work is not an excuse to do nothing. We have been called to grow in the likeness of Christ. That means repenting of our ignorance and tacit approval of the culture as it is. It means embodying the life and ministry of Jesus by standing with the poor, marginalized, and dispossessed, joining our voices of protest with theirs to make sure they are heard. This is certainly not for the faint of heart, and I find myself quoting Isaiah frequently: "But those who wait for the LORD shall renew their strength" (Isaiah 40:31 NRSV).

The reconciling church is also a redistribution center between the haves and the have-nots. For years, John Perkins's CCDA has been a tremendous resource in this area by providing training, consulting, and coaching for the church to go beyond being simply a worship center and instead operating as a center for community transformation. When the reconciling church provides educational tutoring, job training, financial literacy, transitional housing initiatives, or community re-engagement programs for those in need, it serves as a redistribution center of empowerment. When the church prioritizes these principles, it goes beyond commentary about the poor to communal and incarnational solidarity with the poor.

How Should We Understand the Messiah?

The theology and ministry praxis of the reconciling church must also be informed by a Christology that engages the missional and liberating identity of Christ. It is not just about embodying the incarnation but embodying the specific spiritual-anthropological identity of how God chose to be revealed as a human. The Jewishness and social oppression in which God purposely selected to navigate life as human are significant and should continue to inform the church. To avoid exploring and being transformed by the spiritual-anthropological identity of Christ is to potentially worship and project a false image of Christ.

The apostle Paul states that those within the Corinthian church once regarded Christ from a worldly point of view. He also had his own experience of seeing Christ from a worldly point of view. Prior to meeting Christ on the road to Damascus, Paul had been participating in the persecution of the followers of Christ (Acts 9:1-31). He saw Jesus as merely a human being who was a religious and political threat by claiming that he was the Messiah.

Saul met the real Christ and was transformed. He became Paul on that day. Both his name and his life mission were changed. He went from being the persecutor to the one being persecuted. He became a missionary, church planter, and mentor to pastors. By encountering the resurrected Christ, Paul comes to know Christ beyond his humanness. Cone writes of this Christ: "From the outset, the Gospels wish to convey that the Jesus story is not simply a story about a good man who met an unfortunate fate. Rather, in Jesus, God is at work, telling God's story and disclosing the divine plan of salvation."[8]

Paul encounters Christ, and a new story about God and God's mission is revealed to him. Out of the overflow of his own reconciling experience with Christ, Paul becomes a crosscultural, reconciling, and justice-oriented disciple maker. This is shown in his mentoring of a multiethnic young man named Timothy, in his advocacy of women in ministry such as Phoebe, his advocacy for an enslaved man named Onesimus, and his advocacy for accepting Gentile Christians without their need to follow Jewish law. Paul also moves from privileged society to the marginalized. He experiences incarceration and police-like brutality. His life models what happens when one comes face to face with the spiritual-anthropological identity of Christ: one's theology and ministry praxis is transformed. When the church embraces a revolutionary understanding of the spiritual-anthropological identity of Christ, it will discover a reconciliation and justice-oriented theology and ministry praxis.

How the church views Christ affects how it lives out its missional ecclesiology. Specifically, what the church believes about Christ shapes the way it approaches the poor, marginalized, and dispossessed. This, in turn, shapes the church's apologetics because Christology informs missional ecclesiology. The consequences shape how the message of the gospel is conveyed, as either exclusive or inclusive. Examples proliferate today demonstrating how the church continues to view Christ from a worldly point of view—the White Christ, the conservative Christ, the liberal/progressive Christ, the celebrity Christ, and the prosperity-capitalist Christ. These worldly views of Christ have significant influence in American and Western culture. These are some of the false images of Christ that many people who currently attend church may unknowingly be projecting.

Understanding the influence of the White Christ as a worldly point of view will help inform how other worldly projections of Christ negatively influence our theology. The White Christ has historically been the most influential of all the worldly Christ figures in the Western world, particularly in the United States. The White Christ still carries great significance in the racialized and racially divided church today.

The White Christ has been used to justify slavery, the Jim Crow system, and the segregated church. This influence is not limited to the church in the United States but appears to be most deeply embedded within that context. This separation and segregation continues to communicate powerfully to those in emerging generations that the church endorses exclusivity.

The White Christ must be acknowledged and exposed in the reconciling church as the "worldly view" that it is. The worldly Christ has been a divider and an oppressor. The real Christ walked the earth as Jewish, marginalized, oppressed, and yet also liberating and reconciling. The reconciling and multi-inclusive church can begin the process of rejecting the worldly Christ by embracing the Jewish and marginalized Christ of Scripture.

The genealogy found in the first chapter of Matthew provides insight into the Jewishness of Christ. Certainly, Matthew needed to communicate the supernatural identity of Jesus as Messiah. Yet he also wanted to make it clear that Jesus was a Jew, part of a people existing as a marginalized minority group, a subject living under military occupation. The family tree of Jesus was ethnically and culturally connected to a people who had experienced slavery, liberation, wilderness, multiple exiles, and now oppression by the Roman Empire. This genealogy is also not limited to those only of Hebrew ancestry but also includes Rahab and Ruth, highlighting not only the multiethnic makeup found in the genealogy of Jesus, but also a gender-inclusive one at a time when patriarchy was the norm.

This anthropological understanding of Jesus is important because it emphasizes a Messiah who not only brings salvation and transformation to privileged humans like Paul, but to the oppressed, the poor, and the marginalized, as well as those from other ethnic origins. He lives out this mission from the social position of being marginalized himself. This was the heresy and scandal of Jesus for the religious leaders who opposed him. He claimed to be God and King, though he was not born in a community or economic class that was known for producing such leaders. The other part of the scandal was that he offered empowerment and salvation to all people, particularly to the outcasts of society. It is deeply relevant for the racialized and exclusivist reality of today.

Black liberation theologian and historian J. Kameron Carter believes that the Jewishness of Christ can prevent Christians from being held captive to race and exclusivity. This brings realization of the *imago Dei* to those who suffer from racism or are excluded from full participation in the community of God through other means. He presents this opportunity as a mandate:

> And this is the theological mandate: exit the power structure
> of whiteness and of blackness (and other modalities of race)

that whiteness created, recognizing that all persons are unique and irreplaceable inflections or articulations, not of the power/ knowledge nexus of race, but of Christ the covenantal Jew, who is the Image of God, the prototype, and who as such is the fundamental articulation, through the Spirit of God, of YHWH the God of Israel, the one whom Jesus called Father. I mention the Jewishness of Jesus here because of its significance for understanding the I/image of God.[9]

Carter's words here remind us that throughout history, God chooses to be revealed as a liberator and covenant maker who seeks to restore the image of God on all of humanity. This is especially reflected in God's interactions with the oppressed. The incarnation of God in the Jewish and marginalized Messiah is a continuation of the revelation of God and the overarching liberating mission.

The multi-inclusive church must remove all the worldly views of Christ mentioned above and restore him back to his authentic identity as the Jewish and marginalized Messiah, who saves and serves. This spiritual-anthropological identity informs how the church engages and includes the marginalized and poor within their surrounding community.

The Liberating and Reconciling Mission of Christ and the Church

God is revealed as a liberating God throughout Scripture. In Christ human beings are liberated from a life of sin, but also liberated from sinful and oppressive institutions and structures. Jesus receives proclamations of "Messiah" and "King" at the moment of his birth, making it both a spiritual and political event. He disrupts the oppressive religious structures of the day by using the words of the prophet Isaiah to launch his public ministry:

He went to Nazareth, where he had been brought up, and on the Sabbath day he went into the synagogue, as was his custom.

He stood up to read, and the scroll of the prophet Isaiah was handed to him. Unrolling it, he found the place where it is written: "The Spirit of the Lord is on me, because he has anointed me to proclaim good news to the poor. He has sent me to proclaim freedom for the prisoners and recovery of sight for the blind, to set the oppressed free, to proclaim the year of the Lord's favor." (Luke 4:16-19)

Following this pronouncement, Christ's public ministry is to carry out the liberating words of the prophet Isaiah. Christ demonstrates the prophecy through casting out evil spirits, healing the sick, raising the dead, and challenging the abuse of the poor by religious leaders in the temple.

The liberating mission of Christ is salvific and also executes social justice. It calls for the church to go beyond individualistic salvation initiatives to engage in ministries focused on meeting the physical and social needs of the marginalized and poor. The multi-inclusive church is one that addresses all class, social, and racial disparities within its community in some transformative way. Transitional housing programs for the homeless, summer academies for young people below grade level in math and reading, and providing a mobile health clinic are all ways in which the church can and should participate in the liberating ministry of Christ. Crosscultural and justice-oriented disciple makers are the continuation of the liberating ministry of Christ.

Reconciliation is not just the work of God revealed in the Son, Jesus Christ; it is also the message and ministry realized in the work of the church. Reconciliation is foundational to the missional ecclesiology of the church and must be holistic in order to be all that God desires it to be. The beginning of reconciliation is the salvific and social justice work of God in Christ. The growth of reconciliation is the discipling and spiritual maturing work of God in the Holy Spirit. Additionally, reconciliation praxis is the restorative work of God embodied in the people of the church. Reconciliation ministry praxis is the work of God on the whole person and across the whole community.

Reconciliation theologians Curtiss Paul DeYoung and Samuel Hines contend that reconciliation is God's one-item agenda. They challenge the church to put reconciliation at the forefront of their missional ecclesiology:

> Reconciliation with God and each other through Christ is the number one item on God's agenda. Oneness must be realized in the midst of an environment prone to alienation and polarization. . . . Reconciliation brings about peace, both between human beings and God and between individual persons. In spite of all the efforts we make to come together, barriers exist and keep driving us apart. God conceived of reconciliation before the formation of the world.[10]

In Christ, diverse yet divided humanity is redeemed to God and reconciled to one another. The church is given the message and mission of reconciliation, restoring the social connections between people as God intended. God's agenda becomes the church's agenda and informs all areas of ministry life. As those having been reconciled to God through Christ, we become vehicles of reconciliation in a socially divided and unjust mission field. It is the primary purpose of God's church and critical to being seen as genuine in the eyes of many within emerging generations. The separation between God and humanity is not the only place where this transformational work of Christ can be applied; Christ also is the great reconciler among divided human beings.

Jesus shows himself also as a social reconciler, one who desires to break down barriers of exclusivity and separation. In going to Samaria, he deals with the division between Jews and Samaritans (John 4). By engaging with the woman at the well, he opens doors to both gender inclusivity and social outcasts. By putting himself in a position to be touched by a diseased woman, he deals with the division between the sick and the healthy (Matthew 9). His reconciling work begins before he goes to the cross as he purposely steps into the social divisions between Jew, Samaritan, Gentile, the sick and well, male and female, the religious hierarchy and the poor and socially outcast people. Brenda Salter McNeil presents a holistic understanding of the reconciling work of Christ in her book *A Credible Witness*:

> To choose Christ is also to choose his community. . . . As a result of his heroic sacrifice, we are now members of God's family—a new blood-related people group. Men and women, girls and boys, the young and the old, people from different social classes, ethnic backgrounds and religious traditions have been reconciled and are now of the same household. This is the whole truth of the gospel."[11]

This reconciling work of Jesus is given to his followers to continue. Evangelism, discipleship, reconciliation, and justice as the whole gospel is the ministry praxis of the church. This understanding of reconciliation ministry praxis lays the foundation for the equipping and releasing of crosscultural and justice-oriented disciple makers. This is the church that captures the purposes of God for restoring humanity with both God and each other. This is the church that has the power to captivate those within emerging generations who desire to be part of an inclusive and transcendent community working to see humanity restored as God intended.

CROSSCULTURAL DISCIPLE MAKING

The reconciling work of God in Christ is both spiritually salvific and the realization of social justice. Christ's reconciling journey to Samaria is one place of exploration for understanding crosscultural and justice-oriented disciple making. The story of this reconciling journey is found in John chapter four:

Now he had to go through Samaria. So he came to a town in
Samaria called Sychar, near the plot of ground Jacob had given
to his son Joseph. Jacob's well was there, and Jesus, tired as he
was from the journey, sat down by the well. It was about noon.
When a Samaritan woman came to draw water, Jesus said to
her, "Will you give me a drink?" (His disciples had gone into
the town to buy food.) The Samaritan woman said to him,
"You are a Jew and I am a Samaritan woman. How can you ask
me for a drink?" (For Jews do not associate with Samaritans.)
Jesus answered her, "If you knew the gift of God and who it is
that asks you for a drink, you would have asked him and he
would have given you living water." (John 4:4-10)

The reconciling work of God revealed in Christ purposely goes
into the deepest social divides of humanity. Scripture states that
Christ had to go to Samaria, though religious leaders who saw
themselves as the representatives of God took pride in avoiding
Samaria. Salter McNeil describes the deep social divide between
the Jews and Samaritans:

> Samaritans and Jews absolutely did not associate with
> each other. . . .
> Over time hostility between the Jews and the Samaritans
> grew to be insurmountable because of their religious and cul-
> tural differences. The Jews felt justified in their religious, social
> and cultural hatred of the Samaritans who were seen as a de-
> based people—as dogs! To call someone a Samaritan was to
> hurl an extreme insult."[12]

Christ's intentional journey into this socially divisive climate
brings about both spiritual and social transformation. Even while in
Samaria, Jesus chooses to interact with one on the margins of that
society. His intentional connection with those on the fringes communicates the purposes for which he came and the desires God has

for the work of the church. His engagement with the Samaritan woman, along with her discovery of a new purpose at the end of their conversation, is socially transformative. This marginalized and socially shamed woman dares to become a public evangelist in her community because of her engagement with Christ. Her voice, calling on others to meet the Messiah based on her transformative experience with Jesus, leads to many believing in him (John 4:39).

In this engagement with the Samaritan woman, Christ is modeling what a crosscultural and justice-oriented disciple maker looks like. It is a disciple-making moment because the Samaritan women becomes a follower of Christ, sharing her testimony with others. It is also a justice moment because of the marginalization of women and Samaritans in the social culture at the time. In this interaction she is redeemed, and the Samaritan people are restored to being accepted as full participants in the kingdom of God. It is a reconciliation moment because Jesus meets the woman amid her marital brokenness. Jesus as God, Jewish, and male looking up from a sitting position at a marginalized and oppressed Samaritan woman is an affront to the Jewish, male-dominated, religious power structure of the Pharisees and Sadducees. When we connect this engagement between Jesus and the Samaritan woman with the mandate to make disciples of all nations in Matthew 28, we arrive at a more robust understanding of reconciliation theology. The crosscultural and justice-oriented disciple making of Christ is the message and ministry of reconciliation into which each of his followers are called. Ambassadors of reconciliation and multi-inclusiveness must be willing to follow Christ to the people and places that others avoid, crossing divides for the sake of the gospel.

The incarnation of God in Christ both declares and demonstrates the kingdom of God on earth. Eternal life in this kingdom also includes a commitment to inclusivity and justice. For those who believe that individualistic salvation is the only requirement for experiencing the fullness of the kingdom of God, the words of Jesus provide the following wake-up call:

> Then the King will say to those on his right, "Come, you who are blessed by my Father; take your inheritance, the kingdom prepared for you since the creation of the world. For I was hungry and you gave me something to eat, I was thirsty and you gave me something to drink, I was a stranger and you invited me in, I needed clothes and you clothed me, I was sick and you looked after me, I was in prison and you came to visit me." Then the righteous will answer him, "Lord, when did we see you hungry and feed you, or thirsty and give you something to drink? When did we see you a stranger and invite you in, or needing clothes and clothe you? When did we see you sick or in prison and go to visit you?" The King will reply, "Truly I tell you, whatever you did for one of the least of these brothers and sisters of mine, you did for me." (Matthew 25:34-40)

Jesus uses this to provide a picture of the invitation to enter the fullness of the kingdom of God. It demonstrates the expectation to serve the needs of all those on the outside, excluded from full participation. God so identifies with the hungry, the thirsty, the naked, the sick, the immigrant, and the incarcerated that to address their needs is to also serve God.

The incarnation of God in Christ is a revelation of God's solidarity with the poor, marginalized, and suffering. This is not a newly developed projection of what some people desire God to be or an adaptation of some misguided "woke" liberal theology, but the realization of who God actually is and how the church is expected to carry out the ongoing revelation of God to humanity. This fully inclusive understanding of God and the church breaks down the exclusive barriers so demonized by emerging generations and opens the door to seeing them become full participants in God's ministry of redemption and reconciliation. We embrace this understanding not because it might be fashionable with emerging generations, but because this is the message of Scripture and embodies our call to demonstrate God's love unconditionally to all.

FOR YOUR CONSIDERATION

Church Leader: How important has the work of reconciliation been in your local church culture? What evidence do you have to support that belief? If this became a more intentional priority in your setting, what do you think the response might be from current members? What impact might it have on your connection with emerging generations?

Sitting in the Pew: What comes to mind when you think about the main theme of this chapter—reconciliation? Is this something that you believe your church should be focused on? What might that look like and how might this alternate focus impact you?

Millennial/Gen Z: What are the main issues of reconciliation on which you believe your church should focus that would have the greatest impact on your community? From your perspective, what roadblocks prevent your church from moving in that direction? How do you think these might be overcome?

All In: Seeing the work of Jesus and the development of the early church as part of God's movement of reconciliation might be a new perspective. How does this align with your own theology and/or what you believe your church has taught in this regard? How might your church better communicate this theology to help others recognize the need for the church to be immersed in reconciliation?

3

BECOMING THE BELOVED
COMMUNITY FOR EMERGING
GENERATIONS

SIMPLY UNDERSTANDING THE ISSUES the church is facing today does not provide insight into how a local congregation can begin growing younger and more inclusive. This chapter will investigate several specific local contexts attempting to consider what might be necessary to alter the face of the church at the congregational level. The hope is that these examples will provide some encouragement for intentional efforts in other localities. Congregations should use aspects that it makes sense to replicate in their context and gain motivation to brainstorm new possibilities pertinent to their specific region and community situation.

In the books of Acts and Galatians, we find that some of the Jewish followers of Christ believed that the Gentile Christ followers needed to culturally become Jewish in order to truly live as Christians—including, for males, circumcision. The apostle Paul argues that this cultural assimilation takes away from the true gospel and new community that is found in Christ, binding them to the Law of Moses or the cultural expressions of being Jewish:

> You foolish Galatians! Who has bewitched you? Before your very eyes Jesus Christ was clearly portrayed as crucified. I would like to learn just one thing from you: Did you receive the Spirit by the works of the law, or by believing what you

heard? Are you so foolish? After beginning by means of the Spirit, are you now trying to finish by means of the flesh? Have you experienced so much in vain—if it really was in vain? So again I ask, does God give you his Spirit and work miracles among you by the works of the law, or by your believing what you heard? (Galatians 3:1-5)

So in Christ Jesus you are all children of God through faith, for all of you who were baptized into Christ have clothed yourselves with Christ. There is neither Jew nor Gentile, neither slave nor free, nor is there male and female, for you are all one in Christ Jesus. If you belong to Christ, then you are Abraham's seed, and heirs according to the promise. (Galatians 3:26-29)

Scripture shows that the church is founded in the development of a new Christ-centered and reconciling community. This new community is a threat to the flawed social systems and ideologies that divide and place levels of value on people based on ethnicity and the social structure of race. Civil rights leader Martin Luther King Jr. referred to this new community as the beloved community. With this biblical foundation, the true goal of the civil rights movement was birthed out of the African American church and its public theology; but the movement would become ecumenical and inclusive. When King spoke of the vision of the movement, he presented the beloved community. This community is the kingdom of God coming to bear on injustice—this is the reconciling Christian community going public and invading a broken society. The goal was larger than changing laws, for it was the realization of a new community. King often presented this public theology and ministry praxis:

The nonviolent resister must often voice his protest through noncooperation or boycotts, but he realizes that noncooperation and boycotts are not ends within themselves; they are means to awaken a sense of moral shame within the opponent. The end is redemption and reconciliation. The aftermath of nonviolence is the creation of beloved community, while the aftermath of violence is tragic bitterness.[1]

The multi-inclusive church is a Christ-centered and reconciling new community. This kind of new community goes against models of the Christian church in the West that are heavily influenced by the social structure of race, the reality of systemic racism, and an evangelicalism rooted more in the assimilation into cultural whiteness than the transformational and crosscultural gospel of Christ.

One of King's mentors was theologian and mystic Howard Thurman. Thurman was a part of founding one of the first fully integrated churches in the United States, the Church for the Fellowship of All Peoples, located in San Francisco. He hesitated to enter ministry, due in part to his struggle with the racism of the society in which he lived and the racially segregated Christian church that he observed. He wrote of this wrestling that proceeded his planting of a multiracial church in the 1940s:

> My decision to go into Christian ministry came at the end of a period of severe crisis. I could not make clear to any of my friends or my teachers in high school or even to my mother and grandmother the cause of the crisis. As I look back I see that there were three basic elements in it. One, a vague feeling that somehow I was violating my father's memory by taking leadership responsibility in an institution that had done violence to his spirit. Two, the recognition that I could not accept the emphasis upon membership exclusiveness which seemed an authentic part of the genius of the church—the fact that the doctrine of salvation made a gulf between those who belonged to the church as members and those who did not. Three, the examination of the implication of the Christian

ministry upon my life and the life around me, caused the question of the segregated church to become an issue—how could I in good conscience accept it? All three of these questions held me back from the acceptance of the call to vocation. On the other hand, there was the clear pull and insistence of the Spirit of God within my on heart, urging me to say Yes to the Light and to trust God with and for the results.[2]

Thurman's wrestling with the church and his calling into ministry are similar to emerging generations' struggles today. This is a wrestling and questioning about the current state of the Christian church. But to understand the church in much of the Western world as still racially segregated and to envision the development of more multiethnic congregations, it's important to define what makes a church ethnically and racially diverse. In the book *United by Faith,* a group of Christian sociologists and reconciliation practitioners define the multiracial congregation and call for its further development:

> The team spent three years in intensive research, studying both multiracial and uniracial congregations. Relying on studies that focused on when a transitional number is achieved, the team defined a multiracial congregation as a congregation in which no one racial group accounts for 80 percent or more of the membership. . . . Together the four of us set out to answer our question: Should Christian congregations be uniracial and multiracial (or does it even matter)? The result of this search led to our argument—that Christian congregations, when possible, should be multiracial.[3]

The declaration by the team that multiracial congregations should exist whenever possible should be connected to churches missionally representing their surrounding communities. This mission field of the community in which a church exists and the biblical call to make disciples of all nations should ultimately lead the church in striving to become intentionally multi-inclusive. This will call for many existing congregations to embrace change in order to achieve the realization of this new beloved community.

There is often a fear in suggesting change of some long-held tradition, particularly in the Christian religion, that something will be lost, or the gospel will be diluted and no longer represent the message God intended. Yet certain elements of traditional Christian orthodoxy and orthopraxis can be greatly influenced by culture, not always some specific directive of God. Distinguishing between faith influenced by culture and that ordained by God has been a struggle within the church from the beginning, as evidenced by the difficult choices the early church faced concerning the inclusion of Gentiles. All of us should be working to continually distinguish cultural norms from the gospel proclaimed by Jesus. While there might not be universal agreement, we can at least remain open to the idea that not all of our most cherished specific practices are the gospel. In the same way we no longer require circumcision for new believers, we must remain open to alternative ways of communicating to ensure that the message is conveyed clearly to a new generation. "While the nature of God does not change, God's method is adjustable to where people are."[4]

None of the examples that follow are meant to be interpreted as formulaic for successfully diversifying a congregation or connecting with a greater number of those from emerging generations. Neither should these be viewed as congregations who have found success in this realm and are now ready to move on to the next challenge. Each continues to be a dynamic community wrestling in their own way with how best to become the family of God in their unique environment. The examples provided are simply meant to demonstrate the efforts of individual leaders and congregations as they have sought to be more reflective of their surrounding communities, becoming intentionally multi-inclusive environments for faith expression where people are encouraged to grow toward the likeness of Christ.

CITY VIEW CHURCH—JOHNSON CITY, TENNESSEE

City View Church, located in Johnson City, Tennessee, was established specifically to reach those disconnected from faith in the city's downtown. It was launched just a few months prior to the pandemic-induced shutdown by its parent church, which had recognized a need to engage an unreached demographic. It has managed to survive by being intentional about making space for everyone. For Pastor Mickensie Neely, it is important that everyone coming realizes that they have a part to play in building the church. She says, "Church is meant to bring people together from disparate places at a table we have built together."[5] With that simple statement, the emphasis of this faith community immediately becomes a shared space where we are working together to be the church, rather than a program that is put together and polished to attract the "right" demographic.

They realized that current church structures did not work for a significant number of people, particularly those who had previously been injured in some way by the church, or those who had misconceptions about what the church was meant to be. Neely says, "Churches need to be intentional about actively making a space, not just assuming that all people will fit into the space that already exists."[6] This willingness has meant creating spaces not often seen in places of worship.

When they realized that there were families attempting to engage in corporate worship who had children on the autistic spectrum, they set aside space to create a designated stimulus, or "stim," area in their worship center, providing intentional support for their specific needs.[7] They developed a carpeted area with tactile objects and sound-canceling headphones, allowing both parents and students to attend and participate in worship—many for the first time. This simple gesture removed stress for parents who felt judged because their child was "misbehaving" in worship or simply couldn't keep still. In addition, this space has made room for adults who have also struggled with stress or attention issues to feel free to make use of the area themselves. That small area of carpet with headphones and tactile objects right there communicates to parents, students, and any others who struggle to just sit still, "We have space for you, and you are most welcome here."

City View has also sought to recognize that the language traditionally used in the church does not always communicate the same message to different groups of people. Thus, they continue to work to build an alternative vocabulary, or even develop a new faith vocabulary, that better imparts the intended message and helps people grasp the basic concepts from their perspective of origin. Terms understood by many raised in the church, such as redemption, justification, sanctification, and even sin need to be communicated in ways that don't assume prior understanding. Other parts of worship such as confession, baptism, or offering are not readily comprehensible to those not raised in a church setting. Often this means more explanation is needed to facilitate understanding. For those comfortable with tradition this can be unnerving at first; however, it communicates strongly that the purpose is not retaining vocabulary for its own sake but ensuring that the intended messages are received adequately.[8]

For Pastor Neely and this church community, being multi-inclusive is not some form of fence sitting, attempting to make everyone happy, but rather "riding the line of inclusion for all people."[9] The focus questions become, What are the present barriers preventing those in our community from being welcomed? Are there voices that are currently not being heard that need to be? With these questions as a focal point, the community naturally gravitates toward inclusiveness and away from exclusivity.

Even though this church was planted with emerging generations as their target, they have intentionally not adopted the homogeneous unit principle (which we will discuss in chapter four) as a means of attracting a specific audience. Instead, they recognized that much of what turned this generation away from church community was the sense that it was not a place where everyone could belong as they were. There was often an unspoken expectation that church was for certain types of people willing to fit a prescribed mold.

City View Church was planted because there was a need. The intention was that it would grow as a result of meeting the needs of the community in which it was planted. But if it appears that the purpose of a church is simply to grow bigger so that the pastor or founding church can feel good about themselves, it is unlikely to be a very attractive place for many within emerging generations. Antipas Harris writes, "Given the upsurge of suspicion about faith, the Christian mission must not focus on growing churches. It must turn its gaze toward showing the world how Jesus came to love them, affirm their humanity, and offer them hope in despair."[10]

BELOVED EVERYBODY CHURCH— LOS ANGELES, CALIFORNIA

Beloved Everybody Church in Los Angeles, California, takes inclusion to the next level. This church was designated by the Presbyterian Church (USA) as a New Worshiping Community and as such was able to receive special support and some limited funding. Beloved Everybody has created a faith community that is inclusive of those with special needs, physical and otherwise. This requires reimagining everything about how the church functions, including how worship services are conducted and considering what is necessary for eldership.

Bethany Fox, the lead pastor from 2017–2022, believes that the extra effort required benefits everyone. "The point is not creating a church exclusively for people with disabilities, but becoming a place where people connect in multiple ways, thus encouraging growth for everyone."[11] In this way all members of the congregation recognize that they both receive and provide care for one another. No longer is it assumed that the care being given is directed only toward those with special needs. In this community an effort is made to hear and understand God through perspectives normally ignored.

As people gravitated to the small faith community it became increasingly evident that current worship paradigms, such as sitting still for a lengthy spoken message via a sermon, needed to be reimagined if all members were going to participate. Fox comments, "Church is not very accessible to those with disabilities."[12] Most current practices for being the church reveal its limited nature in permitting people with different needs and understandings from full participation. Expecting those with disabilities to accommodate themselves to ensure they don't "disrupt" worship has been the usual approach, even in faith communities that have tried to be understanding of individuals with special needs.

In this new worship space, the pattern of accommodation is reversed. Current members are invited to learn to embrace a completely new worship paradigm more suited to those who have been excluded in previous iterations. "Beloved Everybody casts a wide net for active, sensory worship experiences, creating the feeling of an engaging, contemplative service that goes beyond the limits of most traditional worship."[13] This may mean that messages take the form of artistic expression, worship liturgy may be adapted to provide more inclusivity, community social gatherings will ensure that everyone has the opportunity to participate, and even business meetings have to be conducted through the lens of accommodating people of all abilities. Yet in what other context are those with special needs given the chance to contribute to how the church functions and realize that their understanding of faith is being heard by others?

Fox admits that the development of this church family has been challenging. She believes that some may question why all this effort and energy for such a small faith community are even necessary. Even if one does recognize the need, knowing what is required to make it all happen may appear overwhelming. Yet, she has experienced first-hand that "when someone truly believes in the 'why,' the 'how' becomes more evident."[14] At the very least, the Beloved Everybody church has embraced the notion of inclusivity on a different level than most would even consider. It may not be a large congregation, but for those involved it is transformational and has opened their eyes to completely new experiences of God and faith.

Neither of these two churches is destined to become the next megachurch, nor are they likely to set the precedent for how Christian ministry should be carried out in every context. However, they do demonstrate the efforts of two communities earnestly seeking to bring those previously excluded into full participation in the kingdom of God. These efforts decenter those who have traditionally retained power and influence in the Western church context. When the focus is on inclusion it becomes more difficult to justify the status quo. Harvey Kwiyani understands the importance of this transition: "If we don't have to deal with others different from us, we can easily forget how to be vulnerable with one another. We are not at the center of the universe, therefore we need others to remind us that the center is out there—in God."[15] Thus, the effort to be inclusive creates opportunities for growth among all members, broadening their experience and understanding of God.

For those in emerging generations, the expectation is that their faith expression will be more than simply a passive experience occurring at some regularly scheduled time of corporate worship. This is why many balk at an institution that appears to them to be large on rules and behavioral expectations—yet short on being a transformational force for good in a fractured and polarized society. Even churches working to stand apart from the norm, such as those mentioned above, are frequently tainted with the same brush and are assumed to be just like all the others. Pastor Fox admits that sometimes the moniker *church* is a stumbling block. She says,

"Sometimes we have more space to be the church when we don't use the name church."[16]

This issue is something with which the church as a whole must contend if the desire is to reestablish connection with emerging generations and reflect the inclusiveness of the faith that Jesus proclaimed. Antipas Harris recognizes what this generation is searching for in their religious experience:

> For this generation, religion must touch the heart and not simply mandate rules. Touching the heart goes beyond cozy emotions and speaks to practical dynamics of faith. In other words, genuine religion touches the streets. It champions causes and advocates for justice. It helps people gain a moral compass, discover their identity, and develop gifts.[17]

Much of the challenge, particularly as it regards emerging generations, is that many are confused about what the church is. It can even be embarrassing for many to admit that they go to church at all. Yet, despite what has become the normative way to describe it, church is not something we attend. Church describes who we are. This critical understanding is at the crux of what young people desire to see the church reflect. Despite the recognition that corporate worship is not all that the church does or even is, it is certainly the aspect that generally gets the most attention and in many cases is given the most energy. When one thinks about "going to church," it is almost always understood that this means attending a worship service.

The comments heard after a worship service communicate strongly not only confusion about what church is but also who is the main audience of a service of worship. When worshipers make comments such as "I really liked [or didn't like] the sermon today," or "I thought the music today was excellent [or not very engaging]," it is clear that church is being "consumed" like many other social offerings. It seems that its purpose is to meet the needs of those in attendance and help them feel good about themselves—pumped up and ready for another tough week. When people view themselves as the audience, the ones who are to be satisfied and engaged throughout the structure of worship, it is evident that the original focus of worship has been lost.

We worship an audience of one, the Creator of the universe. Those sitting in the congregation are not the ones to whom everything is directed or whose attention and satisfaction need to be maintained. God is the audience. Those gathered, the congregants, are the worshipers lifting their voices, hands, eyes, and minds to the praise of their Creator and Savior. Changing the consumer mindset may help shift the focus toward ensuring that all participants can freely express heartfelt worship, rather than remaining the center of attention needing to be satisfied. The focus of inclusiveness, then, is not necessarily ensuring that all those in attendance are comfortable or even that they enjoy all aspects of worship. When the emphasis is on God and not on us it becomes easier to accommodate the needs of others, to be open to accepting variety and worshipful expressions different from our own.

Sutton Vineyard—Sutton, United Kingdom

Jason Clark was founding and lead pastor of Sutton Vineyard in the suburbs of London until 2023. He and his wife, Beverly, planted the church twenty-five years ago and have continued to faithfully care for the community through the mission and ministry of this faith community. The demographics of the area have changed dramatically during that time, and while in terms of race it remains largely European, one need only spend a short time there to realize that ethnically it is quite diverse. Twenty-five years ago this was an English blue-collar enclave. Many people now originate from southern and eastern European nations. In addition, there has been a recent influx of people from Hong Kong who have immigrated to the area, fearful of Chinese government policy.

Pastor Clark is quick to grasp the concept of the multi-inclusive church. He recognizes that diversity is not limited to skin tone, which, in the area surrounding his church, would mean there appears to be very limited diversity. Yet it is a completely different story if one uses ethnicity as a basis. He also finds it necessary to remind people who visit his congregation hoping to find a multiethnic church community that they should not mistake Sunday morning corporate worship for the whole of the church. Worship may, in fact, be something that does find greater resonance with those from similar backgrounds or language groups. While that doesn't mean that efforts to diversify worship leadership and worship style do not have merit, it does suggest that one's culture likely influences the freedom one feels to worship fully.

What is certain is that genuine worship does not automatically mean adopting Western Christian cultural norms. If it is recognized that God is Creator of all cultures, then it follows that each culture has unique means of expressing worship of God not found in others. Arguments about what constitutes proper worship and even concerns about syncretism may ensue, but certainly all must accept that corporate worship is not everything for which God created the church.[18]

Sutton Vineyard makes an ongoing effort to help people recognize that they are the church. Once that is accepted they are encouraged to be at the forefront of attempts to be inclusive by asking them the question, "Since you are the church, how can we help you make meaningful connections with people from other walks of life?"[19] Sutton Vineyard encourages its congregants to be active in ministry outside of the church: pursuing issues of social justice relevant to their community, helping new immigrants to the area feel welcomed as they adjust to new surroundings, and engaging in other situations that allows them to be the church in their community, demonstrating the inclusive love of Jesus in as many ways as possible.

In their effort to move beyond the walls of the church, they have been intentional about working with the local city council to help immigrants to the area adjust to the new environment. They have helped to sponsor a Hong Kong festival where police, members of the council, and other local agencies all gathered to help welcome the newcomers, hear their stories, and provide a venue for connections to be made. The work of being the church and facilitating opportunities for its members to be present in the lives of others is, in many ways, far more important than the gatherings that occur on a Sunday morning. When one accepts that the church is not something bound by walls or a place where people gather to worship, it is easier to understand that members' diversity of relationships better reflect what the church is meant to be.

The leadership of Sutton Vineyard recognizes that it is impossible to meet the needs of everyone. This is particularly true when considering corporate worship. However, that does not give anyone the right to demand that their own needs and desires are to take priority over others when it comes to public gatherings. For this congregation, multi-inclusivity is not the sole responsibility of church leadership, nor does it exist so that members can look around a church gathering and feel good about how well-represented different races are. Rather, this church believes that church diversity is more genuine if it is occurring outside of the Sutton Vineyard buildings, as members express the inclusive love of Jesus in their work, school, and home environments.

First Presbyterian Church— Bristol, Tennessee

To look at this church and expect it to reflect fully-fledged ethnic diversity is expecting something nearly impossible. Located in an area where ethnic diversity is almost nonexistent (the surrounding county is 96% Caucasian), First Presbyterian Bristol has still made efforts to be inclusive in ways that fit their community. Recently they hired Jerry Swam Sidi, originally from Nigeria, as the worship leader for their contemporary service. This by itself might be perceived as a form of tokenism, an attempt to project an image of ethnic inclusivity in order to communicate a stronger "hip" vibe than the surrounding congregations. Yet worship leading is only part of his role. He is also tasked with serving the local university campus, working to meet the spiritual needs of the students there.

King University is adjacent to the church buildings and is far more diverse in multiple ways than the surrounding county. Contemporary college students are experiencing all kinds of diversity, even in small private colleges such as this one. They are wrestling with issues of identity and ideology; their views run the gamut on the political spectrum; on top of ethnic diversity present, many are discerning their sexual or gender identities. This gives Jerry and the wider congregation opportunities to meet the immediate and challenging needs of students while they are away from home. These students represent a diversity that can make many in the church uncomfortable, and yet this congregation has seen fit to resource someone to help them navigate this stage of life.

The church's service orientation permits space for students to share their stories, coming from many different regions and nations, backgrounds and experiences. This fosters growth in understanding for the entire congregation. Committing to college ministry will rarely result in church growth either numerically or financially. This is a transient population, present for about forty weeks a year for no more than four years before they move on. Yet making this commitment expresses the belief that the church needs to use its resources to help those in emerging generations continue their faith journey, at a time when many in that time of life are tempted to give it up. It demonstrates a commitment to include people in the faith community unconditionally, expecting nothing in return. It acknowledges that the intersection of their lives with this congregation broadens the vision of who God is and what God is doing in the world.

This congregation has gotten involved in their community in other ways as well. When the local dump began emitting a foul burning odor, causing irritation to eyes and lungs for those in downwind neighborhoods, the church took up the cause to help aid those in need. They have provided dozens of air purifiers to affected families in the region, have attended city council meetings as a strong voice in the community, and are ensuring that their neighbors who often get ignored are heard. Many might consider this outside the scope of what a church should be doing. Yet, if the church is caring for the needs of all of those in their immediate surroundings, both congregants and non-congregants, then they are displaying an important aspect of inclusivity.

WAIKANAE PARISH—NEW ZEALAND

Many of the churches discussed in this chapter have adopted aspects of what is sometimes called the "parish" model of ministry. A parish is a geographical boundary surrounding the church buildings. In times past, this might have been an entire English village or a location within reasonable walking distance. The advent of cars has changed this idea significantly, particularly as cities grow to surround and engulf what were once isolated small towns. Yet the concept still has a great deal of validity; it may provide a better way to think about what the church is and should be in today's fractured world.

Darryl Gardiner is a priest in the Anglican Church of New Zealand based in the Waikanae parish, a short distance north of the capital city of Wellington. He is not a paid staff member of the church but is seen as a volunteer community worker and priest assisting the staff vicar. In addition, Darryl works part time with Kapiti Youth Support, providing mentoring to local young people and supervision for other social workers. He explained that the traditional role of the vicar was mainly not about conducting a Sunday morning service and being available when a wedding or funeral needed to be conducted. "The vicar was acknowledged to be the one responsible for the care of souls within their parish, whether or not the people within those parameters attended worship on a Sunday morning."[20] Darryl's role within the Anglican Church is simply to build relationships with those living in the community, being available in times of need or stress, providing a listening ear or counsel for those who find themselves stuck in some way.

His Christian faith guides everything he does, but his main objective is not to try to fill the pews on a Sunday morning. That would put him in the role of a salesman rather than one who cares for the souls of others. He is quick to point out that "meeting in a hall or sanctuary together is no more significant than gathering in community in other ways."[21] While corporate worship is certainly important, it should not be the primary focus of a church's existence. In New Zealand in particular, where less than 5 percent of the population consider themselves Christian, it would be foolish to assume that God can only be active within the walls of the church. This echoes the sentiments of Barbara Brown Taylor, who says, "I had forgotten that the whole world is the House of God. . . . The House of God stretches from one corner of the universe to the other."[22]

This paradigm of the parish constitutes much of the thinking behind becoming a multi-inclusive church. It means taking a map and drawing a circle with a specific and defined radius around the buildings of a church, and then ministering to all who fall within that boundary. The parish church works to serve everyone as part of the family of God, seeking to demonstrate that God's love is available to all. It may be that few within that radius will darken the doors of the sanctuary, but they should know that the people who gather in those buildings care for them, accept them as they are, champion their battles against injustice, and provide resources for them in times of need. There should be no sense that they are being served so that one day they can be coerced to attend a church service to hear about God. God is already active in multiple ways in their lives;

the role of the church then becomes helping them see where God is already evident in their lives. If in establishing a parish mindset the hope is that one day they will reciprocate and come to church, possibly even contributing to the offering one day, that is a conditional form of love—it will quickly be recognized as false advertising.

Jonathan Wilson-Hartgrove shares the story of one church who began to see themselves as part of a parish, completely changing the way they existed in their community. The congregation began to say, "This is where we are called to set the oppressed free. Whatever is enslaving people, we commit to fighting it by the power of the Spirit."[23] It alters what is considered necessary for the church to function as it should. While a fancy new building may make church more comfortable for those who attend regularly, the priorities might shift if they are more concerned with meeting the needs of those outside the walls than inside them. Wilson-Hartgrove goes on to say, "When church growth isn't about how many people show up for services, but rather how many of the oppressed have been set free, then building a new worship space isn't as important as building a movement."[24]

MIDTOWN CHURCH—SACRAMENTO, CALIFORNIA

The Midtown community is in downtown Sacramento, in the shadow of the state capitol building. Sacramento is one of the most multicultural cities in the United States. Its diversity rivals both Los Angeles and the Bay Area of California. In 2002 Sacramento was named the most diverse city in America by the Civil Rights Project at Harvard University.[25] The population demographic is 45 percent White, 26.9 percent Hispanic, 18.3 percent Asian, and 14.6 percent Black; there are also other ethnic groups moving to the area such as Ukrainian, Russian, and Hmong.[26]

Though Sacramento is very diverse, like other cities, it is facing challenges of racial unrest and disparities. In recent years, many cities have been faced with deep racial tensions. These tensions rose up in Sacramento in 2018 in the aftermath of the shooting death of unarmed African American Stephon Clark at the hands of two Sacramento police officers. The protests that took place in Sacramento in 2018 and 2020 (after the death of George Floyd in Minneapolis) are just part of the broader divisiveness, polarization, and dehumanization plaguing the entire United States.

This city is also experiencing gentrification. It is quite normal to see homelessness and other pictures of urban poverty on one block and a few blocks later see hipster coffee shops and new housing developments. The diversity and disparities offer unique challenges and opportunities for the church. Yet in the heart of Sacramento is a large diverse and inclusive church.

Midtown Church is one of the fastest-growing multiethnic, metropolitan, and multicampus congregations on the West Coast. This community of 3,300 regular attenders has a church demographic that is 35 percent White, 30 percent African American, 20 percent Hispanic/Latinx, 10 percent Asian, and the rest a mix of biracial and multiethnic reconcilers. I (Efrem) am co-senior pastor with Bob Balian, along with our spouses Letty and Donecia, and together we have thirty years of multiethnic, reconciliation, and urban ministry experience. The church staff is very ethnically diverse, with pastors and ministry directors who are African American, Anglo, Armenian, Ukrainian, Russian, Filipino, Mexican, Puerto Rican, Hmong, Korean, and Native American. Midtown Church is making a transformational impact in the city of Sacramento through its ministries to the homeless, addressing educational disparities, equipping marriages and families, and speaking to issues of systemic injustice.

One of the reasons for the success of Midtown Church is that it was initially planted by an indigenous urban leader, co-senior pastor Bob Balian. Balian has lived just about his entire life in Sacramento. He is also well known and well respected within the city; he was a standout baseball and basketball player at Kennedy High School in Sacramento and went on to play at American River Community

College before attending UCLA. He returned home to work for his father's construction business and eventually took over the business. A call to ministry played a role in his decision to sell the business and become a youth pastor in the city of Sacramento. It was from there that he eventually planted Midtown Church (originally called The House Church) after serving as an executive pastor of a large multiethnic church in South Sacramento. I came on staff as co-senior pastor four years into the planting of Midtown Church after planting a multiethnic church in Minneapolis, serving as superintendent of the Pacific Southwest Conference of the Evangelical Covenant Church denomination, and having become president of World Impact, an urban missions and church planting organization. Recently, Susie Gamez, who is Korean and was born in Canada, came on as colead pastor as well. The three of us lead this multiethnic, metropolitan, and multicampus church. We became a multicampus church in 2021, with Tyronne and Raquel Gross planting the Elk Grove, California, location.

The mission statement of Midtown Church, as reflected in the original documents of The House Church, is "to make disciple makers, strategically meet long-term needs in an ethnically diverse community, and plant other intentionally multiethnic churches."[27] This mission is deeply connected to the founding pastor's upbringing in the city and his passion for multiethnicity. Therefore, the church was planted with the following core values:

- Multiethnic: Modeling diversity for other churches and for the city.
- Community Service: Leading the way in compassion and social justice.
- Focus on the Lost: Strategically mobilizing the congregants to reach the lost.
- Exhilarating Worship: Create an irresistible Sunday morning environment.[28]

Since these values go beyond simply the development of a diverse church, this congregation can serve as a reconciling and empowering movement in an urban and multicultural mission field. The original mission statement and core values provide the foundation for developing ministries that can equip and release crosscultural and justice-oriented Christ followers. The goal is to go beyond simply being a diverse worship center to being a community transformation center in a multicultural mission field. Midtown Church partners with its denomination, the Evangelical Covenant Church, to plant multiethnic and urban churches as well as to strengthen African American, multiethnic, and urban pastors. Through a separate but partnering nonprofit, Influential Global Ministries, the church participates in training and resourcing with initiatives such as a leadership institute, a church planting academy, and the Influential Leadership Conference for multiethnic and reconciling leaders.

SOJOURN CHURCH MIDTOWN— LOUISVILLE, KENTUCKY

This church in an urban center of Louisville recognized the changing demographic surrounding their campus, which was still largely made up of Caucasian members. They felt it necessary that the leadership reflect the surrounding community and appointed an African American, Jamaal Williams, as head pastor. This huge step caused significant consternation among many in the congregation, some of whom left the church.

In 2020, the church looked significantly different than in 2016. Sojourn had become a majority white, multiethnic church. However, amid the turmoil surrounding the racial angst, the Black Lives Matter movement, and the death of Breonna Taylor at the hands of police in their city, Pastor Williams recognized that he would have to address these issues from the pulpit. At the height of the angst, Pastor Williams and his preaching pastors preached a sermon series titled The Gospel, Race, and Justice. Though his messages remained biblically focused, even daring to discuss the hurt and questions surrounding the events caused some to suggest he needed to "stick to the gospel" or that he "had lost his way." It was a painful time both for him and the church, especially considering that, like everyone else, they were already challenged by the changes demanded by the pandemic.

But Pastor Williams, surrounded by a strong core leadership team, knew that the church needed to be multi-inclusive—which meant not ignoring the pain that people in the community were feeling. He said that the motivation of all those on the leadership team was to "create the church we most want our children to be a part of."[29] Ultimately, this is what has kept the church focused. They recognize that for children to remain in the faith as adults it will be vital that the church reflect the love God has for all people and be willing to be open about the pain and challenges uniquely faced by each of them.

The move of the church to appoint a person of a different ethnicity from the majority is certainly a bold move, and seemingly much more overt than actions carried out by other churches in this chapter. Yet making such a clear statement demonstrates not only to the congregation but to the entire community that this church is being intentional about making space for everyone, allowing room for all stories and experiences to be shared.

CONCLUSION

These examples have provided a glimpse into possibilities. Each congregation is unique and has sought to convey the love of God inclusively in a way that makes sense to them and their surroundings. Again, the purpose of these examples is not to provide simplistic steps for becoming more inclusive and attracting those within emerging generations. It is possible that working to become more diverse, practicing being the church outside of the sanctuary, and serving those within the radius of a church's parish may be attractive to young people. They may find the notion of the church living as the church is called to live to be what they have been waiting for. But there are no guarantees. The effort to become multi-inclusive is not necessarily to put more people in pews, but to grow the kingdom of God and demonstrate God's universal love for everyone. As Ben Lindsay writes, "As Christians, we are to model the sacrificial, inclusive, impartial, humble approach of Jesus. . . . There is no point in having a loving attitude toward God if we have a hateful or indifferent stance toward people made in [God's] image."[30]

This is how the church becomes the beloved community one congregation, or parish, at a time.

FOR YOUR CONSIDERATION

Church Leader: Which of the above examples represents a context most like the one in which you serve? Are there any ideas discussed here that resonate with how you believe things might work for your congregation? What are some other possibilities to help move the congregation to being more multi-inclusive?

Sitting in the Pew: Which of the examples in this chapter inspire you to consider how your church community could be more inclusive? What might be some of the challenges in implementing these or similar ideas within your context?

Millennial/Gen Z: Of the examples listed here, which do you feel represents the community you would most like to join? What is it about that community that most resonates with you?

All In: Each of these congregations has taken their own unique path toward being more multi-inclusive, and their efforts are different as a result. In understanding the community that surrounds your congregation, who is currently missing from your church and how could you address the barriers preventing them from engagement?

4

THE CHALLENGES IN SEEKING
TO BECOME MULTI-INCLUSIVE

EVEN IF ONE ACCEPTS THE NEED for faith communities to reflect the diversity in their surrounding area, developing and maintaining them is arduous. The idea of what constitutes "normal" church is difficult to alter and frequently maintains traditional, Western European characteristics regardless of denominational distinctions. While there has been some notable growth of multiethnic congregations in the last several years, these are more likely to be new church plants, since altering an established monocultural faith community only adds to the inherent challenges.

This chapter aims to acknowledge several of the inherent problems faced by churches working to become more diverse, adjusting their norms and practices to be inclusive of others. This is deep work, which will never be fully completed. Becoming multi-inclusive is a process by which individual faith communities wrestle with their own biases and acknowledge their own patterns of exclusivity. It represents a consistent effort to open themselves to hearing from those (perhaps inadvertently) excluded and working to make amends where necessary. Ultimately it is a dynamic process to broaden the understanding of God and the family of God, of which all are a part.

But before we present these challenges, let's go back to the idea of "normal" church for a moment. In much of Western culture, expectations and norms around what church should be are largely tied

to the White church. But seldom is the White church recognized by
White people as being the White church. Non-White churches are
frequently described by their ethnic and racial makeup. We have
Black churches, Hispanic churches, and Asian churches. We can
even get more specific as we point to Korean, Sudanese, and
Hmong churches.

But White churches don't brand themselves as White churches,
and some White Christians are offended by the notion that their
churches would be labeled as White. There seems to be either a
denial of the history of the Christian church in the United States or
an ignorance of it. The Black church's history, for instance, is that of
a church forced into existence either by being denied membership
within the White church or receiving a subordinated membership
relegated to church attendance in the balcony of the sanctuary—or
outside the church building.

This has certainly been my (Dan's) experience as a Caucasian man
serving a church lacking much diversity in Atlanta. Our church,
though predominantly White, doesn't use a demographic label; it is
described by its denomination (Presbyterian). There are several
other churches in our neighborhood that are also not diverse, but
they are labeled by their demographics: the African American church,
or the Hispanic church, or the Korean church, even the multiethnic
church. This confirms Efrem's argument here of what constitutes
"normal" church. It is the one to which everything else is compared.

There would be no Black church in America if not for the existence first of a church rooted in a theology and sociology of whiteness.
Whiteness as normative. A whiteness that leads to a White Jesus,
White angels, a White Abraham, and White disciples and apostles in
Scripture, presenting church fathers and mothers as White. This is
the foundation of "normal" church in the United States of America.
Now there were White Christians and churches that spoke against
slavery and other forms of racism in the early history of this nation,
but for the most part, they still carried a White Christianity.

So normal church is White church, whether it is a conservative evangelical expression or a liberal mainline one. But many who attend these churches would not describe their churches by racial makeup. Instead, these churches are described by their denominations, their doctrines, or the style of worship music and dress codes (the overall experience of worship). They are called Bible-believing churches, missional churches, contemporary churches, evangelical churches, progressive churches—but the elephant in the room remains unnamed.

It could very well be the case that without naming the normativity of whiteness within the dominant expression of the American church, it'll be difficult to navigate the challenges that we raise within this chapter. I (Efrem) have been a part of large White suburban evangelical churches where raising the issue of whiteness was met with great offense. In some cases, the offense was followed by a total lack of understanding of what whiteness is. Those who resisted the concept were also unwilling to consider a historical parallel with the early church. In the first century, some Jewish followers of Christ were eager to make Jewishness normative within the Christian church; it was the work of Paul and Peter to broaden the scope. If we embrace this biblical truth and the work of Paul and Peter to create a more inclusive Christian community based on the declarations and demonstration of the true good news of Christ, as well as the words of God to Abraham, we could apply that wisdom to the normativity of whiteness today. We already have a biblical roadmap for the Christ-centered and inclusive church.

Because I (Efrem) am a product of both Black and evangelical churches, I am keenly aware of the normativity of whiteness within evangelicalism. Whiteness and evangelicalism have been connected from the very beginning in the United States. To acknowledge this is the beginning of moving toward a more Christ-centered, reconciling, and inclusive church. Because of the commitment of evangelicals within denominations and other organizations to church planting, church revitalization, and leadership development, evangelicalism offers space for the development of multiethnic and inclusive churches and leaders. But because of its historic and present rootedness in whiteness, if these roots go unacknowledged, evangelicalism can also be dangerous soil for the development of multiethnic and inclusive churches and leaders. I present this evangelical challenge more in depth in my chapter within the book *When the Universe Cracks*, edited by Angie Ward:

> Evangelicalism is not seen broadly as an innovator when it comes to diversity, multiethnicity, justice, and beloved community. How can this be, with what seems to be a commitment to multiethnic church planting and an embrace of racial reconciliation? The answer lies in a conflicting history within evangelicalism of seemingly making a commitment to reconciliation and justice while at the same time promoting and profiting from a White American conservative, nationalistic, and supremacy framework of Christianity. Evangelicalism also has a history of doing ministry in a way that places individual or personal evangelism and discipleship over advancing the Kingdom of God toward both individual and systemic transformation. The preservation of this within evangelicalism becomes the major roadblock for a greater missional credibility in the areas of justice and reconciliation.[1]

In their book *Divided by Faith: Evangelical Religion and the Problem of Race in America*, Christian sociologists Michael Emerson and Christian Smith present some of the problems evangelicalism has faced in this area in recent years and in a more distant past:

> Because evangelicals view their primary task as evangelism and discipleship, they tend to avoid issues that hinder these activities. With some significant exceptions, they avoid "rocking the boat," and live within the confines of the larger culture. . . .

Evangelicals usually fail to challenge the system not just out of concern for evangelism, but also because they support the American system and enjoy its fruits.[2]

Emerson and Smith reveal a contradiction within evangelicalism's journey of justice and reconciliation. Consider one of the founders of the evangelical movement, George Whitefield. This powerful revivalist of the Great Awakening preached the good news of Jesus Christ to Black slaves and supported the institution of slavery at the same time.[3] Evangelicalism in America began in contradiction when it comes to race, justice, and reconciliation.

The Double Consciousness of Whiteness

"Double consciousness" is a term highlighted by W. E. B. Du Bois in the early part of last century. He used it to explain the struggle of African Americans viewing themselves through the eyes of a racist White society. Among those subject to oppression in particular, double consciousness explains the sense that a person's identity is divided into several parts, making it difficult to have one unified identity.

Looking at evangelicalism's justice contradiction, we see a spiritual split within the movement. There are two personalities within evangelicalism, or what Joseph Evans describes as a "double consciousness within Whiteness."[4] This is a White privileged version of the double consciousness that W. E. B. DuBois spoke of within African Americans.[5] And it explains why the current approach to multiethnic church development and racial reconciliation is not working to address systemic racism and racialized divisions in America.

In the 1970s, African American evangelists such as Tom Skinner and John Perkins were received as prophetic voices of racial reconciliation within evangelicalism. At the same time, after Tom Skinner preached a message on racism and world evangelism at InterVarsity's Urbana Missions Conference in 1970, a significant segment of evangelical churches and organizations refused to have him preach or support his ministry. His divorce a few years after the 1970 message was used by some as the reason for many White evangelicals distancing themselves from him, but others point to the Urbana message as the real reason.

In the 1980s, evangelical churches and parachurches began to bring on urban directors and outreach pastors to reach racially diverse neighborhoods and cities. It is within this commitment that my (Efrem's) life was touched as a teenager by ministries such as Park Avenue United Methodist Church, the Park Avenue Youth Leadership Foundation, Young Life, and Hospitality House. At the same time, the evangelical donors to these ministries threatened to stop financially supporting when staff of color, programs, or sermons came across as liberal in their eyes.

In the 1990s, Promise Keepers came on the scene as a mega-evangelistic rally for men, which also called men to racial reconciliation through African American pastors like Tony Evans and Raleigh Washington. At the same time, Raleigh Washington publicly denounced the Million Man March and its focus on inspiring and strengthening African American males. This was possibly motivated by the fear that supporting such a rally might have undermined his status within the evangelical movement.

In the 2000s, books on the case for multiracial and multiethnic church development hit the shelves of Christian bookstores and were featured at pastors' conferences. Major evangelical conferences diversified their speaker rosters like never before. At the same time, after Rev. Michelle Higgins presented a prophetic critique on the state of evangelicalism along with a proclamation that "Black lives matter" at Urbana 2015, some donors threatened to pull their financial support if InterVarsity did not distance some of her comments from the Black Lives Matter organization.

Because of these contradictions, evangelicalism has very little credibility when it comes to being an innovation center of reconciliation and justice. Instead, it is seen as being apathetic toward reconciliation and justice, or even opposed to it. There is a significant segment of evangelicalism that is held captive to whiteness, white supremacy, and white nationalism. This reality shows that changing the perception and the reality of a church movement historically rooted in whiteness takes more than just a commitment to diversity or multiethnicity. There is a need for multiethnic churches whose goal is not simply to look like heaven, but to advance heaven in a broken and sinful world that is plagued by racial division.

The gospel must be presented in its authentic state, including evangelism, discipleship, reconciliation, and justice. With the nation being deeply polarized around issues of immigration, police brutality, mass incarceration, and the sexual harassment and abuse of women, it is important to consider what evangelistic, disciple-making, and missional credibility the church has, even a diverse church. The development of the multiethnic church alone is not enough to bring transformation to a diverse, divided, and polarizing mission field. Therefore, evangelicalism has an opportunity to answer the question, Will evangelicalism embrace a *metanoia* moment and commit itself to the development of crosscultural, inclusive, reconciling, justice-oriented, and disciple-making churches and leaders? The exploration of this question is necessary because an ethnically diverse church is not necessarily a reconciling and transforming church. Diversity alone does not lead to churches that advance empowerment, justice, and multiethnic disciple making.

The multiethnic and inclusive church equips, empowers, and releases crosscultural and justice-oriented disciple makers. Crosscultural and justice-oriented disciple makers will forge unity, transformation, and social justice in their local communities and beyond. They will innovate new paths of evangelism, disciple making, and missions. There is a need for the development of multiethnic church movements that go beyond simply growing visibly diverse congregations to becoming transformational and kingdom-advancing communities.

This process better positions the multiethnic church as a missional force, able to be the transformative solution to the problem of race and racism. This is an opportunity for evangelicalism to truly become a reconciling movement committed to justice and righteousness. This is also an opportunity for evangelicalism to become more fruitful within an ever-increasing multiethnic and multicultural mission field rather than being perceived as adversarial toward it. Acknowledging the normativity of whiteness and committing to biblical justice and righteousness will help churches address the additional challenges to becoming a multiethnic and inclusive church.

There will be many roadblocks, all seeming to prevent change, working against any efforts to grow in this regard. Some of these roadblocks will be universal, experienced by almost all communities seeking to grow in diversity and inclusion. These will be seemingly ubiquitous issues of culture, tradition, and theology, and we will primarily address these challenges in this chapter.

There are likely to be others that may be more specific to an individual context or community; in this space, it is not possible to address all such challenges that a church or leader may face. We hope that addressing some universal challenges will help communities work through their own specific difficulties, knowing that they are not alone. Ultimately, if this truly is what God desires the church to become, then, as communities prayerfully face their own specific biases and challenges, the Holy Spirit will give them the strength and fortitude to press on. The apostle Paul encourages the church in these efforts when he says,

> Not that I have already obtained this or have already reached the goal; but I press on to make it my own, because Christ Jesus has made me his own. Beloved, I do not consider that I have made it my own; but this one thing I do: forgetting what lies behind and straining forward to what lies ahead, I press on

toward the goal for the prize of the heavenly call of God in Christ Jesus. (Philippians 3:12-14 NRSV)

Challenge #1—defining Christian culture. The melting pot metaphor has long been a source of pride for Americans, both in their society and in their politics. While this feel-good rhetoric has served to shape some sense of community and unity, it belies many of the historical facts regarding immigration and the challenges experienced by migrants.[6] For the majority of US history, Europe was almost universally the starting point of those who chose to immigrate.[7] Up until very recently, any that did immigrate from other parts of the world represented a small minority of the total, and often faced even more significant obstacles and racism upon arrival.

Almost all who immigrated faced stiff opposition from those already here. Ethnic tensions were a constant issue during these periods of intense immigration. But, because almost all originated from Europe, within a generation or two they had assimilated into a monoculture of White, Western European ancestry.[8] Many retained idiosyncrasies of their homes such as food or music, but distinguishing one from another in terms of "race" was almost impossible.[9] These peoples "melted" together to create the dominant culture that lasted for more than two hundred years. Thus, the term *melting pot* came to describe the assimilation of many groups into the nation and culture that made up the United States.

Now, however, while immigration continues to provide an influx of new people, the points of origin have changed significantly. Currently, approximately 14 percent of the American population was born outside the United States, predominantly in Asia and Latin America.[10] As a comparison, in 1965, less than 5 percent of the population was born outside the United States—even when accounting for the influx that resulted after World War II.

How has this immigration shift altered the ethnic landscape, and why is it significant? More than 80 percent of the population in the

United States was of European ancestry in 1965. Fifty years later that number decreased to just over 60 percent and is projected to continue to decline, so that within the next forty years there will no longer be a single racial majority in the United States.[11] This change in demographics is driven both by immigration trends as well as consistently higher birthrates in the more recent immigrant communities.[12] Whether or not the United States is truly the melting pot it claims to be will only really be determined in the next fifty years or so.

It is possible that the changing immigration pattern is contributing to the decline in church participation. As diversity continues to become the new "normal," a monocultural worship community becomes increasingly less attractive and may appear antiquated or irrelevant as society continues to evolve. However, this demographic change also provides a fantastic opportunity for the church to become a truly multiethnic community of believers that begins to reflect the vision found in Revelation: "After this I looked, and there before me was a great multitude that no one could count, from every nation, tribe, people and language, standing before the throne and before the Lamb" (Revelation 7:9).

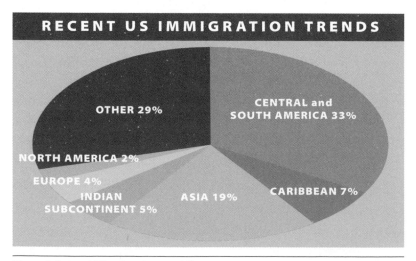

Figure 1. Recent US immigration trends[13]

But the melting pot metaphor does not work well for the church setting. It assumes that all will coalesce together to create one unified Christian culture. What that means in practice in the minds of most is that churches, in worship environments and other communal activities, retain their Western traditional practices, forcing anyone who wants to join to assimilate to the dominant culture. This is how the melting pot worked before; why shouldn't we assume this is how it should be going forward?

But a more appropriate metaphorical picture of what the church could and should be is perhaps the salad bowl, where each individual item contributes to the completeness of the whole while retaining its own unique contribution and flavor. The whole is incomplete, or at least less palatable, without the various distinct contributions. This seems to be more in tune with the apostle Paul's encouragement to the church in 1 Corinthians 12, to see themselves as one body with many parts. But for this important transformation to take place, it will require some significant ideological shifts, as well as a willingness on the part of those currently in power to relinquish it, ensuring that leadership also has a multi-inclusive representation.

Harvey Kwiyani suggests another helpful metaphor: a mosaic. He says, "The kingdom of God is like a mosaic. The beauty comes out of each piece being in its right place and contributing its color—all the pieces, in their magnificent colors, are needed for the mosaic to be a mosaic."[14] The beauty of the church being a mosaic is that not only does it require that each piece contributes to making the whole, but the simile also assumes an artist at work fitting the pieces together. Kwiyani continues: "God is the artist making the mosaic. God is its owner too. Only God can own and make the mosaic—only God has the entire picture of what the mosaic should look like in the end, with the image of God's son revealed through it."[15]

However, the assumption that current traditional church forms are "correct" in representing the way that things have always been done is a powerful force, and difficult to combat. It has meant that many feel that the church does not include them or need them as they are, and that until they are willing to conform to the faith expression of the dominant culture, they are not welcome to contribute. This has maintained the segregated nature of the church and even been used as a tool to grow the church, though not into anything like a mosaic.

Unfortunately, one of the ongoing challenges facing a church attempting to grow more diverse is the relative comfort of those currently in the pews. "Monocultural churches will continue to exist as they are safe, convenient, and comfortable. In a world that rewards those who make the most out of the path of least resistance, the difficult work of crosscultural mission is not very attractive."[16] Yet this is exactly why emerging generations are rejecting the church. If it is safe, convenient, and comfortable, it is not likely to be a place where they expect to experience the transcendent.

Challenge #2—church as business. The church in the United States is considerably more pluralistic than that found in other parts of the world. Much of this is a result of the constitutionally established separation of church and state. What developed, as a latent effect of no state-sanctioned religious institution, was competition for adherents. Churches and denominations have remained in constant competition with one another for adherents and influence. Because they do not have influence or position established and sanctioned by the government, they must attract congregants by any means possible to keep themselves financially viable. In this scenario, traditional practice of the Christian faith becomes a consumer product. This undermines its ability to adequately speak into the culture, for fear that it will lose its status or no longer be economically viable. The writer and poet Wendell Berry pointed this out in one of his many pithy essays, saying, "The organized church is dependent on the economy; it cannot survive apart from those economic practices that its truth forbids and that its vocation is to correct."[17]

What this means in contemporary religious life, as Emerson and Smith point out in *Divided by Faith,* is that "religion in the United

States as a marketplace leads to religious pluralism, increased competition, and a growing emphasis on personal choice. These factors mean that religious congregations need to specialize and market their services to survive and grow."[18] Thus, many churches and denominations have adopted business rhetoric and principles to remain viable. Discipleship is difficult to measure, so attendance becomes a commodity on which decisions are based. It would seem antithetical to spiritual life that this would be the accepted model for discerning success. Yet the global society is inundated with consumeristic values, causing a great homogenization of culture.[19] The church, particularly in the United States, has been swept up in this ideology, falsely believing that this is the means for survival.

In fact, the religious ethos of Christianity in the United States is sometimes described as "the mega-mall of religious consumerism."[20] The myriad options for congregational life encourage consumerism and force churches and denominations that want to survive and thrive to target niche markets. This emphasizes tendencies toward exclusivism and exacerbates church segregation not only by ethnicity, but also by economic and educational status. This leads to the church becoming even more fractured than the visible racial segregation suggests.

Historically, the need to market to niche demographics encouraged the misuse of the Homogeneous Unit Principle (HUP). The HUP is a church growth strategy based around the belief that individuals will find a church more attractive if they share significant characteristics with others in the congregation. Thus, churches are encouraged to target specific, narrow demographics such as young professionals or families with children. The outcome is greater separation and segregation rather than inclusivity and community. This tool was first developed by long-term missionary to India Donald McGavran, who advocated for eliminating as many challenges as possible to Christian conversion on the foreign mission field, including ethnic and language barriers. In the context of missions in

India this made some sense, but it was never McGavran's intent that it would become a permanent emphasis within the wider church.

However, C. Peter Wagner, longtime professor of church growth at Fuller Seminary, reformulated the HUP as a tool for church growth, which was particularly powerful in the market-driven church of the United States. What had initially been segregation as a consequence of racially divided history now became a marketing principle for growing a congregation. Emerson and Smith argue that Wagner hoped to transform Martin Luther King Jr.'s comments on the segregated church "from a millstone around Christian necks into a dynamic tool for assuring Christian growth."[21] While in some notable instances the HUP was effective in growing individual large churches, such as Willow Creek, Saddleback Community Church, North Point Community Church, and others who sought to follow their examples, it did not halt the continued numeric decline in relation to population that has been ongoing since the late 1960s.[22]

In fact, the emphasis on the HUP has only served to exacerbate the segregation of the church in most instances and is the antithesis of what Donald McGavran intended as he developed his missions theory.[23] Early on he recognized that it could be utilized in a detrimental way and cautioned: "There is a danger that [homogeneous] congregations . . . become exclusive, arrogant, and racist. That danger must be resolutely combatted."[24] Those who still believe that the multiethnic church is a better reflection of God's intent for the church as a whole, such as Mark Hearn, argue against the ongoing emphasis of the HUP, suggesting that it "has been misused as an excuse for continuing segregation of churches to prioritize comfort above Christian influence."[25] Comfort was certainly not the purpose Jesus had in mind when establishing the church through the disciples.

The underlying motivation for utilizing the HUP was missional, all based on the emphasis of conversion and evangelism—what were seen as the primary purposes of the church. However, Jesus did not task his followers with converting as many people as possible to their way of thinking, but toward making disciples of himself. Conversion is only one step in the process of discipleship. The HUP prevents discipleship occurring as it should, because it limits the inclusiveness demonstrated by Jesus and fails to acknowledge that all cultures contribute to the full understanding of God's character. HUP altered the definition of what it meant to be a thriving church: from discipleship and community transformation in a context of openness and diversity, to an institution more enamored with and measured by the three Bs—bodies, budgets, and buildings.

The HUP is the antithesis of the parish model of ministry mentioned in the previous chapter. With HUP the objective is to make a church attractive to a specific demographic so that they are willing to drive past multiple other church communities to attend the one that is designed to serve people just like them. This limits genuine diversity and communicates a message far more akin to an exclusive club venue than a welcoming family for all comers. It is true that in many ways it might be easier to maintain niche congregations, which may foster greater job security for staff and provide the affirmation they require. But as Mark DeYmaz proclaims, "Nowhere in the Bible do we get a pass on degree of difficulty. Indeed, we have been called to establish churches that reflect the will of God, not our own."[26] It is much easier to imagine a parish-modeled church becoming a mosaic or salad bowl, as difficult as that process is. Being an HUP-focused church is far less likely to be truly inclusive and diverse because the model is self-regulating.

Church as a business also frequently means that for the "business" to be deemed economically viable, a commitment through membership is necessary. Yet, ideas surrounding what constitutes active membership are also shifting, particularly with those in emerging generations. Mickensie Neely mentioned in her interview how young people feel regarding membership of a church. She says,

Consideration around redefining membership needs to happen. For emerging generations membership represents a contract in exchange for goods or services (i.e., gym, streaming service, ISP, country club, etc.). They do not equate membership with their faith or spirituality because they do not want to attend a church to receive information about God or any other goods or services.[27]

Again, it seems that change is necessary so that the church can fulfill God's purposes for it. Change is not easy. It's uncomfortable. Movement toward multi-inclusive iterations of the church are not likely to grow the church numerically in the short term, if at all. Moving toward a diverse and inclusive church has the potential to open the way for the church to lead Western nations through the polarizing effects of their collective racial and segregated history and reinvigorate the church's place in society when it comes to reconciliation.

Remaining segregated and continuing to pursue market-driven religious consumers fails to live up to what the church potentially could be. According to Zscheile, current practice

> misses an integral dimension of Christian community in a diverse context like that of the United States: The Spirit's reconciliation of people across lines of social difference into a new household of faith. When the church merely reflects social divisions, something vital about its identity and witness is compromised.[28]

Bearing that in mind, one must wonder why the church has not been more willing to embrace a multi-inclusive model. Perhaps a look at some social science theory will provide an answer.

Challenge #3—social challenges of adoption. Diffusion of Innovation Theory (DIT) was developed by Everett Rogers in 1962 to "explain how, over time, an idea or product gains momentum and diffuses (or spreads) through a specific population or social system."[29] He realized that adoption of innovations is a process and does not occur simultaneously within a society. Adoption takes place in a bell curve and means that an individual makes a change in the way they do things as a result of accepting the innovation into their life.

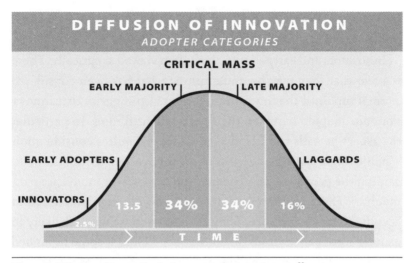

Figure 2. Diffusion of Innovation bell curve—adopter categories[30]

This theory is often applied to explain the adoption of products that represent technological advancement, such as computers, the internet, cell phones, or LED lighting. Rogers argued that there are five categories of people when it comes to adopting innovations: innovators, early adopters, early majority, late majority, and laggards.[31] Whenever an innovation is initially explored, a small minority at the front end of the curve—the innovators and early adopters—explore the innovation and try new ways of doing things. While DIT is frequently applied to material things such as laptop computers or cell phones, it can also explain the use of non-material innovations such as Facebook or Netflix. In addition, it can be used to understand the adoption of social changes such as women's suffrage or the civil rights movement. Thus, DIT may be applied to explain the apparent reticence of the church to embrace inclusiveness in congregations, while continuing in the segregated model that is accepted as the norm.[32] Certainly, the church is rarely viewed as an entity made up of early adopters. Consider how long it took for most churches to accept and adopt digital streaming of worship services and other programs. It was only when the change was forced on it through the Covid-19 pandemic that this technology was widely accepted.

Innovators and early adopters are often viewed skeptically. There is a fear that they may be undermining what has been considered "normal" up until the innovation. Rogers also suggests that innovations are adopted based on their perceived attributes. In particular, the aspect he calls the "relative advantage" requires consideration. When contemplating adoption of an innovation, assumptions regarding the perceived improvement on the current model are paramount.[33] There are also many people who are highly invested in keeping things as they are. They tend to be those who are likely to gain the most benefit from the status quo.[34] Thus, it could be argued that one of the biggest challenges facing the church as it attempts to become more inclusive may be a result of forces within the institution that do not recognize the relative advantage of adoption—or are unwilling to give up their current benefits.

When compared to other institutions such as higher education or the corporate world, the church could certainly be thrown into the DIT category of laggards, who are "oriented towards the past and consistently interact with peers who are similarly traditional as themselves."[35] It appears that the church has been one of the last to respond to and embrace the demographic changes taking place and the need for new, innovative, and diverse expressions of Christian community. Change is something that we should expect. In our conversation, Mickensie Neely noted that we are at the five-hundred-year mark from the Reformation. If history repeats itself, then another upheaval is imminent with tumultuous implications for the church and society as a whole.[36]

As new innovations become part of the landscape, they transform the metrics of success.[37] The accepted norms for gauging success are no longer adequate. For example, as the technology of cellular phones is adopted, a successful telephone company increasingly needs to provide as much cell tower coverage nationally as possible.

At one point in time, the metrics of success had to do with maintenance of telephone cables that crisscrossed the world to provide landlines to all who required them. Now, with few maintaining landlines, this measure of success is obsolete.

Challenge #4—*measuring success.* The Covid-19 pandemic has altered the understanding of church community. The necessary rise in digital tools for broadcasting messages, Bible studies, and worship services to people stuck in their homes has forever changed how people engage with the church. Options for corporate worship gatherings are no longer dictated by geography. Individuals can watch worship, hear a message, or even join a Bible study with just about any church in the world and at any time of the week.

Before, Sunday morning attendance was the standard gauge for determining success. While that may not have been an accurate means of ascertaining spiritual growth and discipleship, it was at least a tangible form of measurement.

But in-person attendance numbers are no longer valid as the sole means for discerning effectiveness. As Jonathan Wilson-Hartgrove writes, the church lost its way when "works of mercy were imagined as auxiliary ministries, dependent on the central mission of building up a spiritual institution."[38] Within the multi-inclusive church context, new measures of success are necessary to help the church measure genuine progress in becoming a diverse and inclusive group of believers. Genuine discipleship of members and meaningful, inclusive fellowship are a more biblical gauge for discerning the value of a faith community. And while gatherings for corporate worship will still be a regular part of what a church does, because there are now unlimited offerings online, other means of being the church must be understood.

It is time to create a new normal—a community full of ethnic, cultural, and social diversity, a mosaic of people all seeking to know God and love others, mostly outside of the church walls. The challenges for this development are significant, particularly because of the forces working against it and the changes that have taken place as a result of the Covid-19 pandemic. Yet, the demographic changes taking place worldwide and the forecast of an even more pronounced diversity in the future leave little room to support any forms of exclusivity or monocultural faith expressions in the contemporary church context. Thus, when church leaders consider the relative advantage for adopting a multi-inclusive church model, they should realize that the monocultural congregational context maintains a significant disadvantage for the local church or the denomination as a whole in the future.

For, as Kwiyani argues, "homogeneity, whatever form it takes, is slow death. A community that builds walls to keep people out [even if unintentional] only imprisons itself within its own walls in the end."[39] Altering this to allow for greater inclusion means dealing with inherent social structures that prevail largely unnoticed. Kwiyani goes on to say,

> A great deal of our understanding of community and belonging reflects the Western marks of individualism and capitalism. That is why [many] denominations find it hard to connect with the lower-class parts of the society. I suspect that an ecclesiology for the economically depressed areas might involve a different dress code from that seen in most congregations. I would also anticipate a different type of language, different musical tastes, and sometime a flexibility around the times of church services, among other aspects of our ecclesiology.[40]

What is also demonstrated in research regarding churches seeking to be more diverse and inclusive is that it is far easier to begin a new congregation with multiculturalism as an expectation than to attempt to change an institution that is entrenched in monoculturalism.[41] Businesses have been better at embracing diversity and training their staff for inclusiveness, but the church engages with issues that are held far more dearly and are significantly more personal than any business venture. The church wanting to be more inclusive of those in its vicinity will need to take a hard look at ecclesiology. In a post-pandemic world, an ecclesiology that does not take into consideration all of these factors will stunt the ability of the church from fulfilling God's vision for it, relegating it to a holdover relic from another age.

Challenge #5—beneficiaries of the status quo. Aside from the racial realities described above, and the recognition that implicit bias provides many privileges to those accepted as White, there are others who benefit from the segregated status quo. We discussed above that, as DIT reveals, some people benefit from maintenance of the status quo. However, it is likely that the long-term benefits may not last as the social milieu continues to change. Those who stand to lose the most in the coming order appear loath to promote adoption of any inclusive change. This appears to be true even within the church.

There is a certain simplicity derived from working in a monocultural context. Leaders have less to consider, do not require continuing education for dealing with diversity, and are not required to engage in any implicit bias training. By contrast, leading in a more inclusive faith community necessitates the ability to relate and communicate in a diverse context.

Most people remain confined and relate to people from similar backgrounds.[42] This limits the level of comfort within diverse contexts and heightens the expectation that people from other cultures need to assimilate if they desire to join the community. Assimilation permits the majority to remain comfortable and eliminates the need to consider how songs, sermons, or newsletters will be perceived by those from other cultural backgrounds. This benefits leaders less able to move crossculturally and permits them to maintain their role in a segregated congregation. If the multi-inclusive church does not become the norm but is simply another fringe option in the church marketplace, then these leaders do not need to change or worry about giving the impression that they have not kept up with the trends. There would be no expectation that they must retrain or grow in their ability to work and communicate within a more diverse context.

There may be a similar benefit for those in the pews. Pablo Morales, lead pastor of Ethnos Bible Church, a small multiethnic congregation in Richardson, Texas, has also experienced the challenges for visitors to his church. In a personal interview, he discussed the verbal feedback he receives from visitors who are looking for a new church but who do not end up joining. He says most come from their own monocultural church experiences and find adjustment to a multiethnic congregation difficult. He says that this difficulty is not exclusive to those from European cultures. In his words, it is much "easier to grow [a church] through new members joining through conversion rather than transferring from other congregations, as new converts do not have previous experience of the monocultural church and therefore have no adjustments to make in a diverse context."[43] Many Christians do not want to have to "work at" community and would prefer to be comfortable in their familiar contexts. However, this perceived benefit may not be valid for those within emerging generations, who tend to be more content in diverse surroundings. The main beneficiaries of maintaining segregation continue to be older adults who are more comfortable being surrounded by people similar to themselves. This may also help to explain the aging membership apparent in many monocultural churches and denominations.

Challenge #6—weak theology. Much of what maintains the monocultural and rather geriatric nature of the church stems from poor theology. The HUP, misused as a tool for church growth, assumed that growth was something that could best be measured numerically. However, the task given to the disciples of Jesus was to "make disciples," and the apostle Paul in his letter to Timothy framed promoting the gospel as predominantly a matter of discipleship (1 Timothy 2:2). The emphasis on considering growth only in numeric terms has only enhanced efforts to engage a niche market and use business and marketing formulas to attract new "buyers."

Pablo Morales decries the focus on attendance as the only measure of growth. He is promoting a new metric of success for the church. He argues that focusing solely on the number in attendance forces the church to entertain, rather than disciple, parishioners. The entertainment paradigm is maintained to attract and keep people in the pews—thus keeping the doors open, the lights on, and the staff in their positions of responsibility. In effect, a parishioner's spiritual life becomes simply another consumable product. Therefore, investment in a congregation will only occur if there are measurable benefits, either in terms of social or emotional well-being, experienced by the individual consumer. Since the pandemic, those benefits are even more difficult for individual "consumers" to measure, as they can engage in what was traditional church from the comfort of their home.

This poor theology suggests that God desires one's comfort rather than growth to become more Christlike. Working through contentious cultural differences is difficult in any context. However, rather than avoiding the challenges and failing to provide a positive example for society, the church should be seen as offering the solution to the polarized society. I (Efrem) believe that too often, churches attempt to address racial and social issues by making doctrinal statements about social issues rather than working toward biblical social justice. But statements are not enough. Members of emerging generations desire to connect to causes and become part of the solutions. Doctrinal statements do nothing to suggest to them that the church has any real intent to change the conditions, unless those statements are reinforced with intentional actions to right the wrongs.

The attempt to simply demonstrate diversity by having so-called people of color in some aspect of front-facing leadership or sprinkled throughout the corporate worship experience to attract emerging generations does nothing to alter the dominance of Western bias or

address the real issues. Pursuit of inclusivity requires far more intentionality in listening to and engaging with varied perspectives. It
encourages an emphasis on exploring areas of bias and not shirking
difficult conversations. It necessitates growing together as unique
members of a community that is seeking to become the body of
Christ.[44] Morales concluded this idea by saying, "Being [a] multi-
inclusive [church] is not external, it is about the core. . . . It cannot
be faked as it is a value."[45]

Ministry director Marcus Bell suggests that a better focus would
be the recognition that the church needs to "pursue inclusion rather
than making diversity the goal."[46] Inclusion suggests a universal el-
ement: that the variety found in all participants would be expressed,
celebrated, and utilized in the communal worship and ministry expressions of the congregation.

Conclusion

It would be easy to be discouraged. "It is not an easy task. True dialogue can be conflictual as we face our own biases, encountering
worldviews different from others. It is to enter dangerous terrain. We
are invited to go 'outside the gate' of our places of comfort and self-
interest."[47] The forces working to thwart a congregation from truly
embracing multi-inclusivity are entrenched, embedded into the
very fabric of the culture, often masquerading as genuine aspects of
faith. Certainly, each of the described challenges would be sufficient
to give pause to any congregation wanting to grow in this way. Realizing that each of these challenges is working in the background
almost in unison is too much to bear.

But congregations are not tasked with tackling all the adversity
described here, as if with some Herculean effort they could single
handedly transform the wider culture. They are called to be faithful
disciples of Jesus, seeking to grow into his likeness and sharing that
journey with everyone around them in the beauty of all the diversity
that exists where they live and worship. The descriptions of the

challenges discussed here are meant to provide encouragement. Discussing these aloud with others and working through them as a community is part of the process of widening the understanding of what the church is meant to be.

The pain of the change may be deep and complicated. Rather than ignoring the pain, it is helpful to allow people to grieve the losses that come with change. The importance of naming the changes, detailing the reasons, and allowing people to speak about their loss is part of the process.[48]

Embracing diversity in this manner will not eliminate or even reduce the problems a church community can expect to face. In fact, if the challenges discussed in this chapter are any indication, working to become multi-inclusive may by some measure increase the problems faced by a congregation. However, if the parish model is accepted as something worthy of embracing, and the mosaic or salad bowl is recognized as a positive metaphor for what the church could and should be, then the process of growing in this form of discipleship should begin without hesitation.

FOR YOUR CONSIDERATION

Church Leader: No doubt this list of anticipated challenges to becoming more multi-inclusive seems daunting. Knowing that these issues are embedded in the culture certainly does not help. How might you help your congregation to recognize some of these issues and begin to consider their impact on developing the church as God desires? Furthermore, addressing the history of the White church is often viewed as political, not meant for church settings. Knowing the importance of continuing these discussions, how might you provide opportunities for church members to continue this process?

Sitting in the Pew: It can be difficult to consider how much of our Christian culture has origins other than Scripture. Which of the six anticipated challenges is most uncomfortable to acknowledge? Which do you think is most evident within your own congregation? How do you think your church might address these to begin the process of removing these barriers?

Millennial/Gen Z: Many in your generation are deconstructing their faith and walking away. Often the issues addressed above are part of the reason they feel Christianity has been invalidated. Have you seen evidence of more genuine expressions of faith less constrained by these issues? How could your church community work through some of these challenges to reflect a more genuine Christian expression?

All In: These are six huge cultural issues for the church. If one accepts that the issues raised above are valid challenges that the church must address, how should they be prioritized? How would you suggest going about helping others begin to understand their impact?

5

HOW THE MULTI-INCLUSIVE
CHURCH WINS THIS GENERATION

BECOMING A MULTI-INCLUSIVE CHURCH is more than a means to the end of attempting to engage the next generation. As important as that is, the motivation to grow more diverse is so that the church, and each individual local congregation, will become a better representation of the full depth and breadth of the family of God. Nor can it be simply a superficial change, highlighting any visible diversity while maintaining every possible detail of Western European orthodoxy and orthopraxis. Not only will emerging generations find this level of tokenism unattractive, but it is likely that it will further drive them and others away from the church's blatant hypocrisy.

So how does the multi-inclusive church win this generation—and, crucially, what does it actually mean to win them? How will transforming the church in this way change the way church is understood, and in what ways will Christian theology develop as a result? Again, it needs to be stated that we are not promoting altering Christian theology to meet the needs of this generation. Theology is in a constant state of flux, as the church seeks to better exemplify who God is and how God is calling the church to work in the world. We simply believe that developing a multi-inclusive theology and acting on it will result in what God has always desired the church to be. At the same time, we strongly believe that living out God's purposes in this way will be a change that those in emerging generations will find attractive.

It is certainly not all doom and gloom. There are churches—those mentioned in chapter three, and a multitude of others—that are working to serve the people in their surroundings, embracing them unconditionally and working to include them as full participants within the body of Christ. If emerging generations are looking for anything from the church, they are searching for a place of genuine community where they can experience and share the love of God as they understand it in the moment.

Each generation has an innate desire to impact the world positively. Few individuals within a generation will find themselves in a position to transform the world around them. People like Thomas Edison, Steve Jobs, Martin Luther King Jr., and Marie Curie loom large and have been instrumental in transforming the way the world functions—so much so that it is difficult to measure. But to suggest that the drive to make an impact is reserved for only an elite minority belies the reality that most individuals innately desire to make a difference in some measurable way.

Those in emerging generations are no different. While many may see their incessant need to seek affirmation on social media platforms as a frivolous waste of time and fear that they will contribute very little to the betterment of humanity as a result, this generation, as much as any previous, desires to be immersed in a cause that matters. These may be issues of social justice, caring for the natural world, equitable distribution of wealth, or whatever else about which they become passionate. Therefore, the Christian faith, and potentially the church it represents, has the potential to connect their passionate demeanor and desire to make a difference with a transcendent faith in God in Christ.

It is true that many within emerging generations are not enamored with much of what the church currently represents to them. To many it demonstrates bigotry, judgmentalism, exclusivity, closed mindedness, and traditionalism. But their frustration with the church does not mean that there are not some aspects of life in a faith community that could resonate with them powerfully. They clearly have a desire for genuine community, particularly after the intermittent isolation and disruption to everyday life caused by the pandemic. While they mistrust much about institutions, they do retain a desire for the transcendent, something that can be experienced in worship. They are generally passionate about issues of social justice and ensuring that everyone gets a fair chance at living a full life, which lends itself to acts of service. Each of these characteristics represents traditional aspects of the Christian faith. Yet these traditional Christian practices also have the potential to captivate this generation if they can get past what they perceive as the huge faults of the church.

In a genuinely multi-inclusive church context, they are likely to experience these things in a manner different from what they may have observed in more traditional, monocultural congregations. In Christian communities that represent the diversity they find in most other aspects of their lives, they can grow out of some of the tendencies toward self-interest. For those who find a diverse congregation in which to grow in their faith, it offers them a place of freedom. Even in Dietrich Bonhoeffer's era, being immersed in genuine Christian community as a follower of Christ meant connecting with the transcendent. He said, "Christ means freedom— freedom from the lie that I am the only one there, that I am the center of the world."[1]

Church, or at least traditional gatherings on a Sunday morning, surrounded by people who look the same and come from similar backgrounds, is not a place in which they desire to connect. But even Jesus never really intended for the Christian movement to become such. Wilson-Hartgrove reminds readers, "If Jesus came to start the church, he didn't have much success in what we think of as typical church meetings. Still, Jesus connected with everyday people and invited them into God's movement."[2] It is the movement begun by Jesus that makes sense to emerging generations—the movement that does not permit exclusion for any reason but demonstrates total love and acceptance for all.

We see this in the Gospel accounts. As Jesus begins his ministry in Luke 4, he is given the scroll of Isaiah and finds the words of the prophet that declare what his purpose will be.

> The Spirit of the Lord is upon me,
> because he has anointed me
> to bring good news to the poor.
> He has sent me to proclaim release to the captives
> and recovery of sight to the blind,
> to let the oppressed go free,
> to proclaim the year of the Lord's favor.
> (Luke 4:18-19 NRSV)

This is the type of mission that will fill young people with a desire to follow Jesus, to engage with the world and connect with their inner longings to make a difference. So, then what are the qualities of a multi-inclusive church that will not only attract them but help shape them into the persons God created them to be?

BROADENED PERSPECTIVE

All of us are influenced by the environments in which we are raised. The people who surround us as children help us form a worldview through which we interpret everything around us. In less diverse communities this worldview tends to be narrow, and even though the ability to use technology to connect with people worldwide is ubiquitous, people tend to isolate themselves in an echo chamber of sameness. But a faith community should be the one place where it is safe to explore important issues with people from a variety of perspectives and experiences. This enables all to broaden their understanding of what God is doing in the world.

Many in emerging generations seem more adept at handling differences of opinion, recognizing that at times these actually shed light on their own narrowmindedness. Working to become a diverse and inclusive community opens opportunity for significant personal growth within a caring and supportive Christian environment. Harvey Kwiyani believes that some tension within diverse groups has the potential to uncover aspects of the mosaic previously unrecognized. He says, "It holds that some differences between individuals and groups are potential sources of beauty, strength, and renewal, rather than misunderstandings and strife."[3] He goes on to say, "Through the eyes of the other we are able to see God in a different light, which always enriches our understanding of God even if we don't agree with what we see."[4] This can be a tough but necessary process, and one in which emerging generations could lead the church if they are permitted.

One means of winning this generation comes from a willingness to admit that maintaining silos of sameness has narrowed the perspective of the church and in some cases been the cause of hurt. Being vulnerable with others different from ourselves, admitting where we have been wrong in our thinking and actions or at least complicit in our silence, is difficult. There may be angst and uncertainty as the community grows to reflect a broader vision of the family of God. Richard Twiss confirms this difficulty but encourages the church to embrace it. He writes, "Mixing is a normative process of positive change and transformation and not always so clear."[5]

It is necessary that we encourage learning and growth outside of traditional contexts. For the gospel to be meaningful it must be contextualized; it must speak to individuals within their own context. When we hear interpretations and understandings from those who come from a different context it can be unnerving. Larry Doornbos, in reviewing the work of Richard Twiss, provides a reason that this remains necessary for the church, even though challenging.

> We need someone who pokes us. Learning from outside is one way the Gospel penetrates our worldview. . . . We of the West,

as well as those of other cultures, are being denied theological insight because of this lack of positive regard and respect for the perspectives of those in other [contexts]. By cutting ourselves off from the insights of people immersed in other [contexts], we of the West are in danger of developing and perpetuating certain culturally-conditioned kinds of heresies.[6]

What the church has often failed to realize is that difference is necessary. Musical depth and harmony do not come from playing only one note. Beauty in visual art or photography is found in contrast rather than similitude. It is variety of color or sound that makes art interesting. It is acceptance of thoughts or ideas from different perspectives that together contribute to the mosaic of community.

Emerging generations are looking for genuine community, one where these difficult conversations are permitted, and redemptive actions occur in real time. Faith communities that encourage inclusivity and allow emerging generations to lead the process will develop a larger understanding and experience of God, even amid the inherent difficulties that this growth will create. Such a faith community will garner enthusiasm from people of all walks of life, encouraged to experience God in fresh ways with clearer vision.

This broadening of perspective is a great opportunity for Caucasian brothers and sisters, where it is still possible to grow up in a very homogeneous world, even if one is experiencing diversity through social media or even by walking around the local mall. This is especially true when it comes to experiencing authority and power. Growing up in Minneapolis, Minnesota, as an African American, I (Efrem) can attest to the experience of living as a minority. Minneapolis has some ethnic and racial diversity but is still a very White city. Though I experienced the authority and power of African Americans through my parents, pastors, and ministry leaders in the Black church, athletic coaches, and some teachers, I was unable to escape the presence, authority, and power of White people. More broadly, as an African American in the United States, I couldn't escape growing up in a world where I had to learn life from the perspective of White people. In many cases, as a person of color in this nation, you must learn how to communicate with and be accepted by White people on some level. To get a grade, make the sports team, get into college, get a job, or get a loan, you must know how to communicate with White people. In this context, people of color have always had to have their perspective broadened beyond their own ethnicity and race. But if you're White, that is not necessarily the case.

Even if a White person lives in a diverse community and interacts with people of color, they may not be in a position where they must change the way they talk, think, or behave because of it. White people don't have to think deeply about having a way that they talk at home and a way that they talk that is acceptable by the dominant culture. It is possible for White people to grow up and not have their perspectives broadened, because they have never had to ask others outside of their race and ethnicity for a grade, permission, a promotion, access, or help. This is about having your perspective broadened through proximity, position, and power. Proximity is where the broadening of perspective and growing crossculturally begins. Proximity is also the way of Christ. Christ put himself in proximity to a diversity of people to demonstrate his broader multicultural kingdom agenda. But being in the same social space doesn't necessarily lead to relational presence.

You can be in a diverse crowd without building authentic community. Presence is about developing meaningful relationships within proximity. This is not just an opportunity for White brothers and sisters, as has already been mentioned. As an African American, I have been proximate to Asian Americans, Latinos and Latinas, and first-generation immigrant Africans at points in my life where I haven't been truly present with them. We need a presence that leads to a deeper intercultural development. A presence that broadens my perspectives in such a way that I am better equipped to make disciples of all nations.

To grow crossculturally I must be present enough to listen, learn, and have any stereotypes and bias I hold dismantled. When I served as church planter and lead pastor of Sanctuary Covenant Church in Minneapolis, early on in our development, we would have multiethnic meals and fellowship with our core team members. I asked folks to bring items that represented their culture and upbringing. We had the enchiladas next to the fried rice, next to the fried catfish, next to the hot dish. We had both sweet potato pie and pumpkin pie at this multiethnic fellowship meal. As we were digesting one another's foods, I challenged us to digest one another's stories, pain, joys, and burdens. Being truly present with each other around tables and having deeper discussions of topics and questions prepared in advance created an environment much more reconciling than just sitting in a diverse worship center on Sunday morning.

The multiethnic and inclusive church also offers an opportunity for more diverse power dynamics, especially for White brothers and sisters who have not experienced power dynamics outside of their own culture. As an African American pastor who has served two multiethnic churches as a senior pastor and one as a youth pastor, I have had the experience of being the first non-White pastor to White members. In these cases, these brothers and sisters had never had someone outside their race in a role of spiritual authority or power in their lives.

The television influence of Oprah Winfrey and the presidency of Barack Obama were turning points for this nation to truly experience African American leaders as leaders for all people and not simply leaders and influencers of Black people. Even with the broader multiethnic agenda of beloved community by Martin Luther King Jr. during the civil rights movement, he was described as a Negro leader. This description was placed on him by the dominant culture not simply because of the racial description given

African Americans at the time, but based on who he was seen as leading. This changed in the era of Winfrey and Obama. Yet because of the lack of proximity and presence to even these iconic figures, non-Black people could choose to live their lives outside of the tremendous influence and power of Winfrey and Obama. I realize that in my role I am stewarding a new kind of leadership with spiritual authority and influence in a post-civil-rights-movement era.

The multiethnic and inclusive church offers proximity, presence, and power dynamics, which can broaden the perspectives of those who are members. As a pastor, my preaching and teaching platform allows me the opportunity to broaden the perspectives of the non-Black people in the congregation. Some of the stories I share, being the son of parents who lived through Jim Crow segregation in Alabama and Louisiana, are ones that some non-Black people are digesting for the first time. They are receiving these stories from someone they have given influence to speak into their lives.

At Midtown Church we have a very ethnically diverse preaching and teaching team made up of men and women representing various cultures. When Russia invaded the Ukraine, our church heard from Pastor Irene Sini-Bailey, who is Russian and Ukrainian. When Asian Americans were facing anti-Asian hate because of ethnic stereotypes and racism connected to Covid-19, Marcella Vue-Pelz, who is Hmong, shared her story on our church podcast. Bob Balian, who I copastor with, is a brother who is Armenian. Another one of our preaching and teaching pastors, Susie Gamez, is Korean. Our youth and family pastor, Gilbert Acevedo, is Mexican. This kind of diversity in positions of power and influence is a great way to broaden the perspectives of those who are members of the multiethnic and inclusive church.

Equipped For a Changing World

The rapidity with which things are changing in the world is difficult to measure. It is hard for some to imagine, but those born after the new millennium have never known a world without the internet, cell phones, Facebook, or streaming services. Their history lessons include the terror of 9/11, the development of the euro, the American military invasion of Iraq, the election of the first African American president of the United States, the devastation of Hurricane Katrina, and the Japanese nuclear disaster at Fukushima. It won't be long until the Covid-19 pandemic will also be a chapter in the history books of students the world over.

How is it possible to prepare for these or other events that cause so much upheaval and alter the way society works? Certainly, being hyper-focused on numbers in attendance at regular worship gatherings has little impact on how well congregants are prepared for what the world of the future may look like. Churches that figure out how to develop beyond passive participation in large corporate services and embody community through alternative gatherings like small groups and other microgatherings will better prepare members for handling the future. It is relationships rather than information that will provide the wherewithal to live through change and upheaval.

Author, pastor, and podcaster Carey Nieuwhof has proposed several church trends in the post-pandemic world that will likely impact the vitality of the church in the future. Several of these are pertinent to the discussion here. He confirms that connecting, rather than gathering, will become a better metric of success; those who put their energy into equipping their community rather than attempting to provide content for gathering will be more effective in the end.[7] Churches and leaders with the vision to create environments where these predictions are able to become reality will find they have far better engagement with emerging generations, as these changes line up well with the desires they have for meaningful community.

Regular worship attendance was already declining before the Covid-19 pandemic. This decline was even greater with millennials and Gen Z. Covid-19 provided a winnowing of sorts. Those who have remained are comfortable with the status quo. One pastor we spoke to believes that those who have moved on either were only engaged habitually and the pandemic broke the habit for them, or they have chosen to seek out a different type of community.[8] It is generally expected that regular attendance in weekly gatherings will eventually stabilize, but it is unlikely that those numbers will ever reach pre-pandemic levels again, and the trend of the future will continue to be a gradual decline. Nieuwhof goes on to say that the reasons for gathering will become more transcendent and the connections within them will need to be more personal.[9] There is far less desire to remain anonymous in a room of people being served information about theological and spiritual things.

As I (Dan) complete the final edits to this manuscript, I am being inundated with texts and social media feeds from Asbury University in Kentucky. They are experiencing a campus revival that began as an ordinary chapel service and has now been five days of prayer, repentance, worship, testimony, and breaking bread. There have been students in the chapel continuously, twenty-four hours a day, while this has been going on. The news about it spread to other college campuses, and many students have traveled hours to join the Asbury community in the chapel. It isn't just an excuse to miss classes. Young people have an innate desire for transcendent experiences, connecting with something bigger and more consequential than their everyday lives. They are hungry to have their faith experiences impact every other aspect of their lives. If they do not find this connection, there are infinite alternatives vying for their attention, most of which have little to do with faith development.

The desire is that faith communities will become centers for deep connection to others, a source of meaningful conversations, meal sharing, service projects, wrestling with important questions, and support through the struggles that life brings. Each person needs to find a place where they are equipped and can contribute.

The multiethnic and inclusive church contributes hands-on ministry praxis models to provide direct connection to many of the social issues going on in the nation in recent years. Midtown Church is committed to deepening its influence and impact within its surrounding community and beyond. At Midtown Church, we are fortunate that the chief of police, city council members, business owners, public school administrators, and professional athletes attend our church. This blessing provides a significant network and opportunity for great influence. It would be a shame for us to look out each Sunday at the diversity of influential city leaders in our midst and not see that as a major opportunity to change the Midtown community of Sacramento. These influential faith leaders are a critical part of the pool of potential crosscultural and justice-oriented disciple makers within our church. Founding pastor Bob Balian, colead pastor Susie Gamez, and I have monthly appointments with some of these influential community leaders.

In recent years, we have worked with Sacramento chief of police Daniel Hahn (who retired in 2021) to improve relations between the police department and communities that are predominantly African American. This was especially needed in Sacramento because of the 2018 shooting death of unarmed African American Stephon Clark at the hands of two Sacramento police officers.

On the evening of March 18, 2018, Sacramento city police officers and Sacramento county sheriff's officers responded to a 911 call stating that an African American male was breaking into cars with a crowbar in a South Sacramento neighborhood. Two Sacramento city police officers came upon a man named Stephon Clark in the backyard of a house nearby. They suspected that he was hiding from police and potentially breaking into a house. Upon calling out to him, they believed he pointed a gun at them and fired shots, killing Stephon.

Later it was discovered that Stephon Clark had no gun, but only a cell phone; he may have pointed it in the direction of the officers simply to show them it was a phone rather than a gun. Also, no crowbar was found to clearly identify him as the suspect who was breaking into cars that night. Even more heartbreaking was that the backyard that Stephon Clark was found in was the backyard of his own grandparents.[10]

The police body camera video released and shown on the Sacramento local news led to weeks of protests by the local chapter of Black Lives Matter and other groups. A town hall meeting put on by the mayor and city council was filled with shouts and cries of anger and deep pain from the African American community and other concerned members of the city. Some of the pastoral staff of Midtown Church attended that meeting, and I had an opportunity to speak.

The death of Stephon Clark revealed a deeper tension between the police of Sacramento and the African American community. The police department of Sacramento, even after the appointment of its first African American chief, is still predominantly White; the makeup of officers is 74.65 percent White and just 3.44 percent Black.[11] Such a disparity, along with little hope of justice being served in the death of Stephon Clark, led to significant racial tensions in one of America's most diverse cities. This really hit home for us at Midtown Church, because at the time, the police chief and his family, the deputy police chief, the grandparents of Stephon Clark, and relatives of the Sacramento County district attorney all attended our church. For almost a year our church addressed the tension between the African American community and the Sacramento Police Department, and the broader issue of race and systemic racism, through sermons, small group book clubs, and online devotionals.

Because of the location of Midtown Church and the diversity of those who call the church home, we had no choice but to be involved in this issue. We talked about this in sermons and in pastoral observations during the announcement time within the experience of worship. We hosted town forums and used this time of deep tension in our city to create bridges of reconciliation and understanding. We used this moment of division to present the biblical call provided by the apostle Paul in 2 Corinthians 5 to serve as ambassadors of reconciliation. We also explored the overarching narrative of righteousness and justice in the Bible. We challenged our church and invited them into practical ways of living out reconciliation, righteousness, and justice.

One of the practical ministry opportunities we invited our church into was our partnership with Leataata Floyd Elementary School in an underresourced section of Sacramento. One might ask, "What does that have to do with tensions between the African American community and the police?" Well, from resources such as Michelle Alexander's *The New Jim Crow* and information shared by the Children's Defense Fund, we found the connection. When urban children in underresourced communities are at grade level in math and reading between the third and fifth grade, they are less likely to be incarcerated and more likely to go to college. This also correlates with being less likely to be shot and killed by police officers. Of course, this does not take away from the need for police reform; but it does provide an opportunity for engagement in a very tense issue for a multiethnic and inclusive church. Midtown Church partners with Leataata Floyd School, providing Chromebooks and internet access to students during the pandemic and running a summer school academy and a summer day camp. We are dismantling the pipeline to prison and opening the gateway to college.

In 2020, we experienced the trinity of social unrest with the deaths of Ahmaud Arbery, Breonna Taylor, and George Floyd; the Covid-19 pandemic; and the highly polarizing presidential campaign between Donald Trump and Joe Biden. But it was the death of George Floyd that truly exposed not only racial unrest in the country but also the racial divide within the body of Christ. This also created a unique opportunity for the multiethnic and inclusive church.

Just by being in the heart of Sacramento, Midtown Church was in proximity to protests and riots. Yes, we made statements, but we also participated in a solidarity march with police officers, pastors, and community activists. We invited speakers to our church for midweek gatherings to address the history of racial bias and systemic racism, specifically in the state of California. Because George Floyd died on the block I grew up on in South Minneapolis, I shared my own story along with another African American Sacramento pastor, Rev. Dr. Tecoy Porter of Genesis Baptist Church. We launched new small groups based on a book club model featuring books focused on racial reconciliation, biblical justice, and systemic bias and racism. On one hand we dove into these initiatives because of our founding mission and vision. But on the other hand, we launched these initiatives based on what we were hearing from the young adults and teenagers in our church and surrounding communities. During these initiatives we heard comments such as "Midtown is real in this community!" and "Midtown is out here where it's going on, and they hear us!"

These examples show how Midtown Church worked to equip our members to engage the brokenness around them and find ways to serve as reconcilers and justice-oriented disciple makers. Each congregation will need to respond to the changes and issues affecting their neighborhoods. Such work will often be messy. It will frequently challenge church leaders to develop outside of their comfort zone. There may be a sense of isolation as other congregations in the area choose to maintain the status quo. But as disciples of Jesus, we are called to be the agents of change that he declared when reading from Isaiah 61 as he launched his ministry. This is the type of church emerging generations hope to find, one that connects their experiences in the church buildings with the lives they lead outside them.

DEMONSTRATING RADICAL LOVE

There is a strong hunger for relationships that are genuine, mutually gratifying, and that offer opportunity for diversity in terms of gender, ethnicity, and even age. The church is an ideal context for such relationships, but many congregations appear averse to moving away from the pursuit of a niche market in the misguided hope that it will

help them grow numerically and maintain fiscal viability. Rarely in
the polarized society that constitutes much of the Western world are
there places to experience the uncompromising love attested to in
the New Testament. In our personal interview with him, Jamaal
Williams expressed as much regarding the connection between
emerging generations and the multiethnic church: "[The contemporary church] should offer a context for the radical expressions of
love as demonstrated in the early church that would be especially
attractive."[12] That radical love should be occurring within the multi-
inclusive church and be stark in contrast to that which is often seen
and experienced in other contexts.

Despite the greater diversity evident in younger generations, they
will not be easily enticed into relationships that may challenge aspects of their self-awareness, as true crosscultural relationships may
do. Though they are certainly more comfortable with diversity than
previous generations, people mostly continue to be drawn to those
much like themselves and are not often strategic in the pursuit of
multiethnic relationships.[13] But a community that is willing to challenge one another toward greater understanding of the diversity
within God's creation, be vulnerable as forgiveness is sought and
given, and therefore experience a radical form of love that is unique
in the world, will be captivating to many and worthy of the investment of time and energy. For many in emerging generations, the
cost of something defines its worth or value.

One way of thinking about this radical form of love is like an arranged marriage. People in an arranged marriage have not been swept
up in the romance of a courtship or felt their heart beat faster when
they lock eyes with that attractive person across the room. In an arranged marriage, the relationship occurs because of the mutual commitment of families. Mason Okubo explains further: "Being in a
[multi-inclusive] church community is a little like being in an arranged
marriage. We didn't choose the cultures we were married to. We were
married because, through faith, we were all adopted by the same

Father, redeemed by the same Savior."[14] That is the type of radical love commitment that can result from intentional microgatherings in a multi-inclusive church context. Korie Little Edwards writes,

> [Multi-inclusive] churches are to be places where every person's belovedness is embraced and celebrated; where every person is able to come to the table with their gifts and skills as leaders and contributors to advance the Good News of Christ; and where no form of supremacy other than the supremacy of Christ, reigns.[15]

As a pastor of a multiethnic and inclusive church in California, I (Efrem) am moved by the types of relationships and communities that are formed. Through our prayer ministry and our small groups ministry, not only does the picture of diversity do something to my heart, but the witnessing of crosscultural relational depth is amazing. On our prayer leadership team, for example, the inclusive DNA within allows brothers and sisters to share about the various expressions of prayer from their own cultural perspective. Some think of prayer expression such as intercessory prayer from the cultural perspective of evangelism, others from the perspective of righteousness and justice, and others from the perspective of spiritual warfare. Each member of the team is invited and empowered to bring these cultural understandings of prayer to the table and develop a more inclusive prayer ministry model. What brings us together in the midst of the diverse cultural perspectives is our willingness to receive from one another and our collective belief in the authority and centrality of the Scriptures. This allows us to grow as a Christ-centered, biblically-rooted, and multi-inclusive prayer team.

ALLOWING THEM TO LEAD

This generation will also be inspired if they are given the opportunity to demonstrate leadership. It is a difficult transition for the older generation to relinquish control of how things happen. It

means that changes will be instituted that make older adults uncomfortable at times. The strongest leaders will be those who can
speak in the multiple "languages" necessary to communicate to
everyone. This is usually not something that can be learned, but is
an intuitive aspect of growing up as a bicultural kid. Consider the
process of older adults learning to use a smartphone. They don't
turn to their spouse for help, but rather their children or grand-
children. These kids know how to operate the technology, as well as
how to communicate to the adults about its use.

As the culture continues to evolve, younger people understand it
innately and how to explain to previous generations what is occurring. This is where bicultural communication is key for the
church. The only ones capable of doing that well are young people.
It means that if the church is going to evolve, emerging generations
must be given the opportunity to lead those changes, helping to
transform the church into a body better able to engage with its
altered surroundings.

"Keychain leadership" is a term developed by Kara Powell and her
team at the Fuller Youth Institute. It describes the willingness of
those holding all the "keys"—of access, decision making, strategic
planning, and critical roles or authority—to hand over the keys and
empower multiple people in areas of leadership, including those
within emerging generations.[16] Often those leaders who fail to share
leadership for various functions of the church are concerned with
controlling what is produced and need to feel that they themselves
are critical to the success of any venture. But the willingness to involve people at multiple levels, to encourage those currently in roles
of passive participation toward invested responsibility, fosters a
sense of ownership and belonging that is particularly attractive to
young adults. The results of research by Faith Communities Today
verify the assumptions behind keychain leadership. They found that
emerging generations have a stronger commitment and connection

to congregations when they receive multiple opportunities for involvement in addition to weekly corporate worship.[17]

This validates the idea that emerging generations desire to be more actively involved in their faith than may have been evident in previous generations. The authors of *Neighborhood Church* bear this out: "[Emerging generations] seek a way to incarnate their passions: passion for a just world, passion for a less judgmental church, passion for service that actually makes a difference, passion for a sustainable lifestyle."[18]

Keychain leaders who recognize these desires, and empower emerging generations with opportunities to manifest them and lead others in the same, are far more likely to garner their commitment in all aspects of congregational life. Experiences are a powerful teacher and can be used by church leaders as means of discipleship and spiritual growth. As John Seel suggests, emerging generations "take their views from life, not authorities."[19]

This need for the experiential corresponds with what Efrem has described as the church's two-pronged focus to engage emerging generations. He said that the church must be committed to spiritual development as well as engaged in social causes that young adults care about. For them, engagement with a faith community requires both of these concurrently. Developing these areas synchronously will likely help retain those who already have some form of God-frame while also attracting those who are unchurched but are cause oriented.

This is why engagement with social justice issues must be more than simply doctrinal statements, but also provide actual opportunities for experiential immersion. This two-pronged emphasis is not suggesting that churches need to consider developing more programs. The primary concern should be about shaping lives. Finding contexts where relationships can be fostered on some form of common ground will reduce the need to develop something new.

The African American church, and specifically its involvement in the civil rights movement, is a great missional example of young people being empowered for transformative leadership. It was middle school, high school, and college students who were on the front lines of the civil rights movement with Dr. Martin Luther King Jr. and other pastors in the 1950s and 1960s. It was girls like Ruby Bridges, who risked her life to integrate schools in the Deep South. It was college students who sat at lunch counters and were spit on, yelled at, and had hot coffee thrown at them. We consider these children and teenagers young heroes for God, giving of themselves to change a nation based on beliefs they learned in the church.

But empowering young people for leadership was not just a civil rights movement strategy. It's a biblical one as well. The Bible is full of children and teenagers empowered by God for leadership. David killed Goliath as a boy. Josiah became a king at eight years old. A teenage girl named Esther became a queen and risked her life in approaching the king to advocate for her people. A teenage girl named Mary gave birth to the Savior. A teenager named Timothy was prepared by Paul to be a church planter and apostle. If only the church saw in young people what God sees.

At Midtown Church, we are leaning deeply into this challenge to see young people the way God does. We have teenagers and young adults on leadership teams of just about every ministry of our church. We are not just committed to being a multiethnic church but also an empowering, intergenerational church as well.

Conclusion

The multi-inclusive church will win this generation if it is willing to look beyond its traditions, embrace the concept of living in radical love, and celebrate the diversity—created by God—in its midst. This does not mean that all forms of church tradition should be eliminated. We simply have to be willing to consider their intended purpose and if they still communicate clearly in this generation.

Many traditions continue to be important ties to the foundations of the church. There will also have to be a willingness to hand over leadership to those whose experience of the world comes from a different place but who nonetheless desire to share the gospel effectively in the new environment.

Perhaps pursuing the multi-inclusive church community is simply misguided hope; perhaps this generation is already lost, and no amount of transformation will sufficiently change the church into becoming something that will meet the needs in this new age. But to be paralyzed, afraid to do anything for fear that the little that remains will be lost, is resignation to inevitable decline. There remains hope for this generation and hope that the church can grow to become a meaningful contributor to fractured communities and broken individuals everywhere. That is a cause worthy of investment.

What is certain is that if the church remains static, unwilling to evolve or grow, it will only exacerbate the exodus of emerging generations. That won't necessitate the death of the Christian faith per se, but will certainly speed up the decline of the institutional church structure.

FOR YOUR CONSIDERATION

Church Leader: There is much to be gained by listening to the experiences of those within emerging generations. They have different perspectives and experiences that will be important to lead the church into greater inclusivity. Efrem provided multiple examples of how his church is immersed in the community and thus engaging emerging generations. Where could your church find opportunities to confront the systemic issues in your community? What steps could you take to demonstrate to them how the church can be the catalyst for change, not only in the community but in their own lives as well?

Sitting in the Pew: Engaging emerging generations is critical for the future of the church. Yet the church can win this generation and be transformed by committing to become a reconciling and inclusive institution. Which of the aspects listed in the chapter headings seem most achievable to you? How do you think your congregation might respond to the actions of Midtown Church, as described by Efrem?

Millennial/Gen Z: How do you feel about the work of Midtown Church? Is that the type of Christian community you feel those in your generation need and/or desire? What are the issues in your area, and how could your congregation be engaged like Midtown? How can you provide some leadership for helping your church in this way?

All In: The multi-inclusive church has the potential to bring renewal to hurting communities. It can also be an institution that emerging generations recognize as critical to bring healing and reconciliation. This could change the perception in their minds of what the church stands for or chooses to overlook. What are the issues in your locality that should be addressed by the church? Where are the opportunities for listening to the stories of others?

6

WHOSE IDEA WAS THIS ANYWAY?

IN RECENT YEARS THE CULTURAL DISCOURSE has been filled with the need to encourage diversity and inclusion. Many see this as part of a progressive agenda determined to undermine the foundations of society and, even more threatening, infuse conflict within the Christian church. However, perhaps, transitioning the church toward something more inclusive is part of God's plan, and not unruly progressivism.

Although the Christian faith, taken as a whole, is the most diverse religion in the world, individual faith communities infrequently reflect this reality. Most churches represent their own unique enclaves of ethnic, social, economic, educational, and theological mono-culture. Many within the church, however, fear that the move toward inclusiveness is just the latest in a long line of progressive attempts to weaken the structure of the church and dismantle its ability to positively impact the culture with the gospel. Yet the penchant toward exclusivism evident within individual churches is not the intent of God as expressed in the Bible.

Certainly human communities have tendencies toward exclusion. Yet, uniquely, the Bible consistently exposes God's inclusive nature and the Creator's desire that divine restoration be experienced by all of humanity. Malcolm Patten is convinced that without a doubt, "the affirmation of people of all nations is an important biblical and theological foundation."[1] Scripture demonstrates the desire that humanity, in its entirety, be restored to full communion with God and that this be universally expressed in the diverse communities that result. This is a biblical expression of inclusiveness within vibrant faith communities, breaking down barriers that have kept people apart for generations.

However, to accept this vision of the inclusive church, it is necessary to recognize it as the church as God desires. This understanding will only come through sound interpretation of the biblical record. The Bible will not provide specific tools for becoming a more multi-inclusive church. It will provide the foundation for understanding God's desire that the church be a community incorporating people from all walks of life.

Over the course of the historical development of the Bible, human tendencies toward exclusivism were consistently overshadowed by God's theme of diversity and inclusion. The original orators, writers, and later redactors and scribes not only understood that this text was a divinely inspired message but also recognized God's universal love for all people. This is consistently communicated even though people in these communities may have preferred to limit the Creator's inclusive nature to those more like themselves.

The Hebrew Scriptures demonstrate this beginning with the establishment of the Israelites through the initial Abrahamic covenant, then expanded on in the Mosaic law, and later experienced through various narrative accounts of God interacting with people apart from solely the Israelites. In the New Testament, diversity and inclusiveness are evidenced in the life and teachings of Jesus as he eschewed the exclusive biases of the religious leaders of his time. It is also found in the early church in the sometimes-tense debates regarding the requirements for Gentile believers to be accepted as full participants in the Christian faith.[2] The miracle is that, despite the human tendency to exclude, ultimately God's inclusive message as found in Scripture prevailed through millennia of oration, inscribing, translation, canonization, and interpretation.

At the same time, when anyone interprets Scripture, there's a tendency to read it through one's own cultural biases, which are different from those of the original author or the intended audiences. For most in the Western world in the twenty-first century, that severely limits understanding, because the perspective through which Scripture is being interpreted is strongly individualistic and materialistic and missing powerful concepts of mutuality and a spiritual domain.[3]

Twenty-first-century readers also often assume that the Western European church is the normative church. This lens is often inappropriately applied to events described in the Hebrew and New Testament Scriptures. This means that contemporary readers often miss the evident cultural diversity present in the texts. Realizing this, Patten argues that it is crucial to remember that "the biblical world never existed in a monocultural bubble but was always challenged and enriched by the ethnicities of those around or within."[4] This is true of all of the accounts contained within the Old and New Testaments.

The biblical record not only demonstrates God's universal love for people from all walks of life; it also highlights the diverse way God interacts with people from various cultures. This affirms that the way people worship and relate to the Creator is not limited to specific, culturally defined practices or narrow ideological stances. The desire of God, relayed through the biblical texts, is complete restoration of the divine relationship with humanity, replete with the created cultural diversity. As the relationship with the Creator is restored it facilitates the ensuing healing of the human community, one with another. Investigating the Scriptures through that lens will confirm God's desire for human thriving.

Old Testament—The Hebrew Scriptures

The Israelites believed themselves to be the chosen people, God's elect, called out and separated from all other peoples by design. Much of Hebrew Scripture gives testament to this belief. Yet there remains a clear and consistent theme of God's universal love for all of humanity and a sense of obligation on the part of the Hebrews to communicate God's concern for others.

The Covenant and Law in the Pentateuch. Beginning with the covenant with Abraham, God expresses the desire that through the Israelites as descendants of Abraham, "all the families of the earth shall be blessed" (Genesis 12:3 NRSV). Patten clarifies God's intentions: "Here it is explicit that the blessing of all nations on earth is the intention, even as one family, which will become the nation of Israel, is favored to accomplish this end."[5] The key to this understanding is the recognition that in the Hebrew text the word for "families" echoes the Hebrew word used for the descendants of Noah and his sons found in Genesis 10, often referred to as the table of nations. Daniel Carroll builds on this understanding: "So, whatever else the call of Abram might entail, at the very least one can see that it is designed to reach to 'all' the peoples descended from the sons of Noah."[6] Abraham and his entourage have their first encounter in a land occupied by Canaanites. Shortly after this they are forced by famine to live as aliens in the land of Egypt. It seems that God wasted no time in communicating circumstantially the full intent of the covenantal blessing, and that isolation and separation from others was not part of the equation.

The full scope of the covenantal blessing continues to be unveiled throughout the life of Abraham. After the prophecy that Sarah will bear a son, God tells Abraham that "righteousness and justice" are part of God's blessing to be demonstrated by Abraham and his descendants (Genesis 18:19 NRSV).[7] This covenantal purpose highlights the understanding that at least on some level, the Hebrew people recognized that God had called them for the sake of others—not simply to lavish love on them at the exclusion of outsiders.

Of all the Old Testament texts one might assume would be bereft of inclusiveness, the Mosaic law, which defines and establishes the Israelites as a distinct nation, would seem most likely. These laws are the basis of Hebrew identity and provide a distinct connection between them and God. Yet even here the basis for inclusiveness is evident, and the realization that various people groups are to be accommodated and included in the Hebrew community is codified.

Central to the Law of Moses are the Ten Commandments, those initial statutes given by God, which communicate a new way of life for the Israelites. However, Rolf and Karl Jacobsen suggest that, because the commandments are so familiar to modern readers, what is often overlooked is "how often God's concern for the welfare of the neighbor is prioritized. In fact, it is not too strong to say that the main point of the Ten Commandments is God's concern for the welfare of the neighbor."[8] Even the commandment for Sabbath, which might appear to be more concerned with an individual's maintenance of religious custom, is directed at the head of the household to ensure that all within their household are provided a day of rest, including children, slaves, and alien residents. "But the seventh day is a sabbath to the LORD your God; you shall not do any work—you, your son or your daughter, your male or female slave, your livestock, or the alien resident in your towns" (Exodus 20:10 NRSV). God's intent for the Hebrews was to establish community, and it was anticipated that it would include people from all walks of life and cultures. In addition, it is apparent that God desired that all should be included in the expressions of community as laid out in the law.

The attention to the neighbor only begins in the Ten Commandments. Leviticus is where the bulk of the Hebrew Law is codified. Chapter 19 of Leviticus is recognized by scholars as an important section of legal instruction. This chapter "not only forms the center of chapters 18-20 of instructions, but also the entire book and the Pentateuch as a whole."[9] In Leviticus 19:18 we find the familiar command to "love your neighbor as yourself." The term "neighbor" here is understood to mean "one like yourself," meaning human, not the person who lives next to you. The definition of what constitutes a neighbor is fully clarified only a few verses later in verses 33 and 34:

"When an alien resides with you in your land, you shall not oppress the alien. The alien who resides with you shall be to you as the citizen among you; you shall love the alien as yourself, for you were aliens in the land of Egypt" (Leviticus 19:33-34 NRSV).

David Smith believes this is significant:

> While verse eighteen speaks of loving one's neighbor with members of Israel in view, a few verses later, in verse thirty-four, the 'love ___ as yourself' formula is repeated with a significant change. The command is now "Love the foreigner as yourself," and is reinforced by reference to Israel's founding experience of the Exodus, before which "you were foreigners in Egypt."[10]

The Israelites as a people have experienced being outcasts and foreigners. In light of their own history as aliens, they are therefore called to care for those in their midst in a manner that highlights the "righteousness and justice" God tasked Abraham's descendants to display in the covenant.

Central to the interpretation of the law found in Leviticus is the importance of maintaining holiness. This understanding is not limited to worship practices, sacrifices, or other temple requirements, but encompasses many other aspects of daily life. Hendrik Bosman, a South African professor of Old Testament studies, makes a convincing argument, saying,

> Loving the neighbor and the stranger involves special kinds of creative acts that open up new and transformative spaces and relations in all regions of social life, usually divided by race, economic class, gender orientation and religion. Holiness is thus achieved not through exclusion or separation but by an inclusive attitude, thereby including those different from [oneself].[11]

This theme of inclusiveness is consistent throughout the Old Testament and is highlighted in comparisons of the righteous and unrighteous found in the Psalms and the Prophets. "One of the ways in which both the Psalms and the Prophets characterize the wicked is in their treatment of their neighbors."[12] The idea that righteousness according to the law is exhibited by the love demonstrated toward those outside one's family group testifies to the fullness with which these laws had been accepted by the Israelites. These "outsiders" were generally understood to be the most vulnerable in society and included the widows and orphans as well as aliens or strangers.

To be clear, for the Hebrew people, how to "love your neighbor" was broadly interpreted; but, to practice evil or wickedness was clearly expressed as taking no care for the welfare of those who are vulnerable. One could argue that the focus was on issues of justice more than pragmatics. Yet this aspect of the law demonstrates the humility required to live in community and the willingness to alter one's attitude toward those who are different. God's judgment of the Hebrews is often the result of continued arrogance toward their neighbors, as highlighted in Jeremiah 9:6. In this verse the prophet suggests that the mistreatment of the neighbor is a sign that "they refuse to know me, says the LORD" (NRSV). This is a

> telling critique of Israel, and potentially those of us who read these texts as normative and authoritative. In both the Psalms and the Prophets there is an expectation that the Pentateuchal laws will be in play. We are called, even commanded, to love our neighbor; to not do so is to show that we are not like the righteous. To fail to love our neighbor is to show that we "do not know the way of the LORD, or the law of our God" (Jer 5:4).[13]

There are also examples of God's desire for including outsiders in the narrative portions of the Old Testament.

Narrative examples in the Hebrew Scriptures. It's the lives of those found in the other Old Testament books, including the historical, prophetic, and poetry books, that provide the fuller meaning and application of the law for contemporary circumstances. Even today, the characters described in Scripture have much in common with our lives because of the shared human experience. Thus, the Old Testament offers a great opportunity to understand God's desires regarding how people are to relate to one another and join together in diverse community. There are too many different events to discuss all of them, so key examples have been selected for the unique perspective they provide.[14]

Second Kings 5 tells the brief but puzzling story of Naaman, who was the commander of the army of the Arameans. He had recently defeated Israel in battle and taken a young Hebrew girl as a slave. In his need for a cure from leprosy, he accepts the advice of his newly acquired Hebrew slave girl to visit the prophet Elisha for healing. In this account, God demonstrates care for outsiders, even those fighting as enemies of the Israelites. Ultimately, Naaman is healed from leprosy; he then attests to the reality of Israel's one true God, who is evidently "active through both a non-elect leader of Israel's enemy and an Israelite slave girl."[15] The interaction with the prophet Elisha is limited, but no Hebrew worship practices are required prior to the healing taking place. Naaman himself apparently found this frustrating, and though he ultimately recognizes the sovereignty of YHWH, there is no indication that he becomes a Jew or relinquishes his military fight with Israel.[16]

The book of Jonah is unique in the Hebrew Scriptures, in that "with the sole exception of the main character, no Hebrews appear, and the Gentiles are the focus of at least half of the book."[17] While the book is named after the main character, it is apparent that the intent of the writing is partially to communicate the universality of God's favor. Jonah runs from God not because he was afraid of speaking to the Ninevites but because he feared that they would receive God's message to them. He feared that this would lead to their repentance and then God would ultimately display mercy toward Israel's enemy. Again, as in the story of Naaman, there was no requirement that the Ninevites convert to Judaism, be circumcised, or adopt any other Hebrew practices, either before or after receiving God's mercy. This suggests the story of Jonah is confirming "God's plan of redemption has, in his mercy, always been global in scope."[18] In fact the implication is that the Hebrew law was superfluous to restoring the Ninevites, highlighting the mercifulness of God regardless of ethnic background or religious heritage. In reality, "by their response to the prophetic warning, however ephemeral it may have been, the Ninevites put hard-hearted Israel to shame."[19]

Other examples of God's clear inclusiveness of people of other cultures are evident in the Prophets. Amos chastises Israel for their arrogance:

Are you not like the Ethiopians to me,
O people of Israel? says the LORD.
Did I not bring Israel up from the land of Egypt,
and the Philistines from Caphtor and the Arameans from
    Kir? (Amos 9:7 NRSV)

The implication is that God is not limited by the Abrahamic covenant with the people of Israel. They are reminded that God has been active in the growth of other nations and peoples. Walter Brueggemann writes, "What happens in this striking assertion is that Israel's monopoly of YHWH is broken. This does not deny that Israel is the primal recipient of YHWH's powerful, positive intervention; it does, however, deny any exclusive claim."[20] The implication is that God takes an active role in the circumstances of all nations and cultures. It may also communicate that though the worship practices of Israel and Judah were the best means of experiencing God, they were not necessarily the only means. As one considers the challenges of developing diversity and multi-inclusive faith communities in the contemporary church, the realization that there are potentially multiple ways to express devotion to and experience God provides impetus for the deconstruction of exclusively Western forms that remain entrenched in much of the Christian world.

By the time of Jesus, the Hebrew Scriptures were largely canonized. Gentiles were received into the faith as God-fearers, and proselytes and the diaspora had created a faith that included members from across the Roman Empire.

The teaching and ministry of Jesus, and the eventual development of a new religion, were going to turn things upside down. Someone claiming to be the Messiah had come and would reassert God's desire that all are welcome in the kingdom of God. A look at the New Testament is necessary to understand the emphasis toward inclusiveness that Jesus promoted and the early church's interpretation of that teaching as it began to form and grow.

NEW TESTAMENT—THE TEACHING OF JESUS AND THE EARLY CHURCH

Jesus completely disrupted the status quo of the Jewish faith community in first-century Palestine. Throughout the course of his ministry, he performed miraculous signs that gave credence to his claims of divinity. He challenged those in authority and provided alternative and authoritative interpretations of Hebrew Scripture. He also connected with people from all strata of society, and ultimately generated a significant following of common people as well as a small group of disciples. While his main purpose was redeeming humanity through his sacrifice on the cross, all his interactions with people demonstrated a broader inclusiveness than previously experienced in the Jewish faith.

How does one understand the essential purpose of the ministry of Jesus and the trajectory of the Christian movement that followed regarding inclusiveness, diversity, community, leadership, and acceptance in the kingdom of God? Like all Scripture, the teaching of Jesus is open to interpretation. And while the demonstration of

God's inclusiveness is one focus of Jesus' ministry, many have used Scripture as a means to exclude.

Therefore some questions need to be investigated.

How did Jesus alter the understanding of inclusiveness in his own time?

What are the implications of that for the contemporary church?

How does the development of the early church provide insight into the life and teaching of Jesus around the issues of inclusiveness, leadership, and community?

New Testament scholar Emerson Powery writes, "The role of the Bible and its interpretation were significant in the developing traditions of religious movements and sectarian groups of the first century, just as they are for contemporary Western society."[21] Therefore, there is an ongoing need for this work so that the contemporary church can continue to grow to fulfill God's intentions for these communities of faith based on the life of Jesus.

The development of the Gospels. Each individual Gospel writer includes events that suggest that the work and ministry of Jesus was fostering an inclusiveness that was revelatory, completely different from anything that had been promoted previously.

For example, only in Mark's gospel does the author have Jesus describe the temple as a "house of prayer for all nations" when Jesus is upturning the tables in the temple (Mark 11:17). This is a message not picked up by the two remaining Synoptic Gospel accounts. It is only in Luke that the author records Simeon's declaration at the initial presentation of Jesus at the temple that he will be "a light for revelation to the Gentiles" (Luke 2:32). The Gospel of John alone describes the interaction of Jesus with the Samaritan woman at the well, which is significant both for the fact that the individual is a woman and also Samaritan. And in the Gospel of Matthew, the author begins with a genealogy that includes not only four women but specifically Gentile women, again making a clear statement about the undeniable heritage of Jesus that highlights his diverse family background.[22] While these individually unique insertions occur in different instances in the life of Jesus, their uniformity of theme is noteworthy.

Even the purpose for writing each Gospel may have been influenced by the need for inclusivity and community among diverse believers. Individual Gospel authors wrote to a specific audience and for purposes unique to each context. Yet the theme of inclusiveness is consistent throughout. This further attests that the Holy Spirit was guiding this motif through each author's writing.

The Gospel of Matthew specifically contains a pluralism that directs attention to the context in which it was written. It is this Gospel that most succinctly defines the ministry of Jesus for the purpose of announcing the presence of the kingdom of God. This kingdom was not to be understood in the traditional sense where only certain people could be included or counted as citizens, as was the case within the Roman Empire in which they lived. Matthew has Jesus declaring this kingdom to be inclusive of all humanity.

Most scholars suggest that the Gospel of Matthew originates from Antioch following the Jewish war of 66–70 CE. This community likely included native Antiochian Christians, Jewish Christians fleeing Jerusalem, and Christians from other parts of the empire who had either permanently taken up residence or were part of the trade mechanism of the city. Thus, it was imperative to join together this diverse community by highlighting the inclusive nature of the ministry of Jesus. Carson Reed argues that Matthew used the theme of God's kingdom defined by Jesus to unify the Christian community in Antioch. "In contradistinction to the imperial empire, the heavenly empire (kingdom), as witnessed in Jesus's words and ministry, orients and shapes the operative focus of congregational life."[23]

The Gospel of Matthew represents an effort to draw together the diverse threads of the congregation and unite them by recognizing the true community to which they all belonged, the kingdom of

God. Carson Reed again believes the focus of Matthew points to a leader in the midst of a challenging and somewhat chaotic context, but also

> suggests a congregational leader with plenty of urban issues, marginalized narratives, and ethnic diversity in play. Yet steadily and consistently, from the very opening of the Gospel, Matthew astutely connects with varied constituencies and invites them into the richly imagined world of Jesus's proclamation—"The Kingdom of heaven is at hand."[24]

Matthew is not alone in efforts to draw together a disparate community of believers from the diverse geographical and political contexts where scholars locate the text. Yet, it should be recalled that this Gospel account is frequently described as the most Jewish of the four Gospels. Notably, however, within its highly Jewish perspective is found this emphasis on inclusion and diversity in the kingdom. This demonstrates what the church should seek to become.

Jesus and inclusivism. It also must be acknowledged that some events in the Gospels appear to represent the antithesis of inclusiveness and care for one's neighbor.

Many might be quick to remember Jesus' encounter with the Syrophoenician woman in Mark 7. In this discussion he responds to her request that her daughter be exorcised by saying, "Let the children be fed first, for it is not fair to take the children's food and throw it to the dogs" (Mark 7:27 NRSV). The suggestion is clear that his work is with the Hebrew people and not outsiders. Amy Levine, author of the Jewish Annotated New Testament, is convinced that the use of the term "dogs" here is a "highly insulting name as dogs were regarded as shameless and unclean."[25] Though Jesus does exorcise the girl based on the faith of the mother, in spite of his desire to "feed the children [of Israel] first," this interaction does not show any inclination of Jesus to develop an inclusive ministry for the sake of outsiders. Yet at

the same time, much of his ministry did broaden the scope of understanding regarding acceptance into the kingdom of God.

Within the Gospel accounts, it is evident that Jesus did not
conform to many of the religious ideologies of his time. His se-
lection of disciples, who had likely been passed over by other rabbis,
is one example.[26] In addition, his acceptance of people whom religious leaders found wanting, such as Zacchaeus, the woman caught
in adultery, and the Samaritan woman at the well, demonstrates his
religious nonconformity. Furthermore, several of his parables feature
characters considered "outsiders" in the Jewish religious framework.
All these examples connote an inclusiveness unlike that of his religious contemporaries. Many found Jesus engaging, but it seems that
he attracted an unusual crowd of followers, evidenced by the re-
action of the religious leaders to his ministry. There is much
agreement that "Jesus' disciples and the crowds who gathered
around him are, by the most positive reading of the Gospels, a
motley crew."[27]

These things all suggest a form of ministry that was attractive to
those who found themselves excluded by the religious elite of first
century Palestine. Jesus was not unique as a rabbi for maintaining a
group of disciples and followers. What was unique in the ministry of
Jesus was the way he selected his disciples. They were not the well-
bred or intellectually elite young men who would be probable
candidates. He chose those who had already been overlooked for
discipleship and had instead begun their adult lives as tradesmen.
This set the stage for the type of people he would attract and the type
of ministry he evidently intended to develop. Dorothy Weaver writes:

> The people who associate themselves with Jesus of Nazareth
> reflect vivid diversity on a variety of fronts: class, gender, life-
> style, ethnicity, and ideology. These people are not carefully
> screened for compatibility with one another or even for their
> likelihood of success as followers of Jesus.[28]

These actions were intentional, designed to provide a pattern for his followers to carry forward when his own earthly ministry concluded. Lenny Duncan, addressing the segregated nature of the contemporary church, finds in the ministry of Jesus purposeful provocation: "To believe that Jesus didn't understand the political ramifications of his actions belittles his ministry and reduces it to something sanitized and safe."[29]

In addition to his choice of disciples and the motley group of people who followed him, it's the interactions Jesus has with outsiders that demonstrate an exceptional inclusiveness and clear desire to communicate his purpose to restore all of humanity to full communion with God. The most powerful is his engagement with the Samaritan woman at the well found in John chapter four. Of all the groups that could have been highlighted, it is the Samaritans that the Jews found most unappealing. As the Broadman commentary points out, "Even Jews who showed reasonable tolerance of other races were openly contemptuous of Samaritans as half-breed descendants of the former ten tribes of Israel whose racial purity had been corrupted by foreign settlers."[30] The fact that Jesus even chose to pass through Samaria demonstrates his unwillingness to maintain the cultural social conventions of the Jews of his generation. In fact, his motivation for traveling here may have been a further signal of his ultimate intention toward inclusiveness. Potentially, "in traveling through Samaria, Jesus was not merely looking for a shortcut to Jerusalem. Rather, he was on a difficult path of reconciliation; he was extending an olive branch—a hand of friendship to the Samaritans—the supposed enemies of the Jews."[31]

Though the disciples were in the city during the initial interaction between Jesus and the woman, they no doubt witnessed the crowds that she brought to meet Jesus and were later informed of what had previously occurred between them. Considering the cultural constructs of the period and recognizing that the disciples were all Jewish, events such as these served to alter their own

perspectives. Though they did not know it at the time, these unusual interactions would frame their understanding as they began
to bear witness to Jesus as the Christ and establish the church, eventually communicating God's plan to include all people.

Jesus also makes a point to highlight the legal Scripture from
Leviticus 19 discussed previously. His use of this passage highlights
its centrality to Jewish understanding of the time, but also emphasizes his desire to challenge the exclusive tendencies of many of his
contemporary religious leaders. By using this passage, he connects
himself to the challenging words spoken by the Hebrew prophets of
the eighth century and underscores his "ethic that is love-driven and
inclusive" rather than based solely on correct religious observance.[32]
It is a "rejection of ritual acts of worship in favor of theologically
sound, ethical behavior."[33]

In the Gospel accounts, Jesus never mentions the expectation of
the law to love "the alien who resides with you" (Leviticus 19:34
NRSV). The Jews of his time understood themselves to be indigenous to Palestine, but they were once again subjects of a foreign
empire, and likely believed they had more in common with the
alien in Leviticus than the authoritative native suggested in the
verse. However, beginning with the Sermon on the Mount, Jesus
takes the Leviticus laws of neighboring and "broadens the meaning
of neighbor to include enemy, a step beyond loving the alien."[34]
The challenge becomes a willingness on the part of colonized
Jews to "love your enemies and pray for those who persecute you"
(Matthew 5:44), an even more difficult proposition than loving the
alien as found in Leviticus.

In addition to his interaction with the Samaritan woman, Jesus'
discussion with the Jewish lawyer, found in Luke 10, provides him
with another opportunity to draw the circle of those accepted by
God much wider. The discussion centers on the understanding of
neighbor found in Leviticus, and Jesus again includes a Samaritan,
in an unanticipated way, this time as a character in his parable.

While the lawyer was most concerned about justifying himself and defining his responsibility toward others, "Jesus shifted the focus from the lawyer's question, 'who is my neighbor?' to Jesus's concern, who acted like a neighbor?"[35] This transforms the discussion by highlighting the unexpected concern exhibited by the Samaritan in response to the injured Jew in the story.

Jesus makes powerful use of the ethnic tension surrounding Samaritans to drive home his desire that the lawyer and those like him "should stop asking who his neighbor was in order to set up a neat list of exclusions, and instead set about being a neighbor, even across religious, ethnic, cultural, and political boundaries."[36] This is the crux of much of the teaching of Jesus. He was providing a new interpretive framework that fostered inclusiveness rather than exclusiveness. As in the account of Naaman in 2 Kings, God's desire is exemplified through "outsiders," eliminating the boundaries so entrenched in the religious culture of the time and opening the way for receiving all who will ultimately be included in the kingdom of God as the church becomes established.

The four Gospels intentionally highlight diverse followers who surrounded Jesus during his ministry, retell specific interactions that demonstrate the expanding inclusiveness of God's people, and use the stories that he told drawing on Old Testament interpretations of the law. All of these set the disciples and early church toward "negotiating cultural boundaries, establishing a trajectory for others to follow a mission of breaking down barriers between people."[37] Even as Luke describes the ascension of Jesus this emphasis is strengthened, as Jesus further reminds the disciples of their role to witness "to the ends of the earth" (Acts 1:8). This confirms their responsibility to continue to fulfill the Abrahamic covenant to be a blessing to all nations.[38] It also prepares them for the role they would play in communicating this good news in a multitude of settings.

THE FIRST-CENTURY CHURCH

We must also consider how the trajectory of inclusiveness that began with the ministry of Jesus was interpreted in the early church. Thus far we have demonstrated "how Jesus shifted the emphasis toward reaching out to those of other ethnic and cultural backgrounds [which] inevitably led to the early church becoming a multicultural community with all the intercultural issues that arose."[39] However, these efforts within the early church were not without their challenges, and though Luke did his best to show a unified and uniform movement in the book of Acts, there are several instances of difficulty mentioned in the book, in addition to those suggested in the Epistles. These all indicate that while diversity was growing in the new faith communities, it did not occur without considerable tension.

It seems that even within the very early church in Jerusalem, at first almost entirely Jewish, there was misunderstanding stemming from the cultural distinctions that were a part of the community. The apostles struggled to come to terms with the rapid church expansion occurring through the conversions to faith in Christ. At the very least, at this time, there was linguistic diversity, with both Aramaic-speaking Hebrews and Greek-speaking Hellenists worshiping within the same faith community.[40] The apostles begin to receive complaints from the Hellenist community that their widows were not being treated fairly in the distribution of food. It seems that the huge numbers of conversions to the faith post-Pentecost were difficult to handle and that the fellowship of believers was only just beginning to unravel the practical implications of this new community life.

Acts and the Epistles testify that even with significant goodwill and the joy evident in this newfound faith, "life is still messy, and prejudices and patterns of power do not shift overnight."[41] It seems that the ongoing challenges of developing a genuine faith community made up of people from disparate cultures and backgrounds are a permanent aspect of the Christian faith, even with concerted attempts to live out the will of God.

As the movement quickly spreads to far-flung parts of the Roman Empire, the diverse nature of the individual faith communities grows. Each local branch of the church is influenced by the surrounding culture as well as the various ethnic groups and social classes that made up the new converts.[42] Incredibly, "these communities were remarkably diverse for first century social or religious groups, and that diversity seems to have been a source of both great creativity and also no small conflict."[43] Yet despite the challenges of maintaining positive relationships in and among the new local churches, there was evidently significant effort made toward networking with other members of the faith in multiple locations.

It was these intentional connections, even with the inherent cultural and language barriers, that encouraged the sharing of the early epistles with Christian congregations throughout the Roman Empire. While there was an acceptance of the authority of the mother church in Jerusalem, there was also significant autonomy. Each community was permitted to participate and offer their unique perspectives regarding the questions surrounding what it meant to be a believer. These networking efforts "involved various activities, among them the sending and exchanging of texts, believers traveling for trans-local promotion of their views, representatives sent for conferral with believers elsewhere, or sent to express solidarity with other circles of believers."[44] These efforts are in addition to the several examples of financial support for the ministry of the apostles and specific faith communities in need.

The growing acceptance of maintaining a diverse faith community was also evident in metaphors used by Paul, highlighting the need for the church to be inclusive rather than exclusive. This most clearly appears in his use of the metaphor of the body in his letter to the church of Corinth in 1 Corinthians 12. Some scholars believe that this illustration is not simply highlighting the various gifts and roles that individual members may bring to a faith community, but is testament to the influence that the growing diversity of adherents had on understanding the life of Jesus and how to live as a follower. It is suggested that the individual body parts mentioned in the text are a means Paul uses to continue the unifying message of the gospel and deal with some of the conflict that has arisen as a result of the interpretive tensions.[45]

The effort to understand God's purposes did not mean that the church was to eliminate diversity in order to maintain peace or force some form of assimilation. This distinction becomes clear when Paul's unifying themes are understood.

In Galatians 3:28 and Colossians 3:11, Paul directly and clearly addresses the explicit differences that so often serve as a source of division and difficulty. He is not declaring that in Jesus Christ those distinctions are now obliterated. Rather, they should no longer separate people. In the body of Christ, ethnic (or diverse) identities are maintained, and they contribute to the beauty of the body.[46]

Even within the leadership of the church, there seems to be an emphasis on sharing responsibilities and permitting all members of a fellowship to contribute in worship. Despite the diversity evident in the early church, Paul exhorts the community in Corinth to anticipate that each can expect to contribute in some manner, though he attempts to establish guidelines to maintain some order.[47] Evidently, however, these informal structures were part of the expectation of the imminent return of Christ, and thus were usually not sustained much past the first generation of the church.

In time, a more structured approach to community life began to develop, particularly with the affirmation of the Christian faith by the Roman Empire early in the fourth century. This marked a turning point, as the undeniable ethnic diversity of the early days was replaced by a Gentile Christian majority in a matter of a few decades.[48] However, with each successive generation, the faith continued to expand and infiltrate unevangelized parts of the world. While some of this growth included significant enculturation, the mandate evident in the biblical canon to "be a blessing to all nations," to "love the neighbor and take responsibility for the alien," and to communicate "God's love for the world" all serve to emphasize the expectation that God's desire is for all people to be included in the kingdom and participate fully in the community that results.

This inclusive expectation is ultimately summarized in the book of Revelation. At four different times the author underscores the desire of God for all people that was expressed in the life and work of Jesus (Revelation 5:9; 7:9; 10:11; 14:6). In each instance the entirety of humanity is included, and no distinction is made between who they represent. "None are included because their ethnic or cultural identity makes them superior; none are excluded because their ethnic or cultural identity makes them inferior."[49] Revelation shows a church that is transformed into an inclusive community, no longer bound by the previous understanding of what constituted the "chosen people of God."

> No longer is status as God's nation based on membership within a specific ethnic group. Now people from the entire world are called together to belong to God; the church is an international fellowship comprising persons "from every tribe and language and people and nation" (Rev. 5:9).[50]

CONCLUSION

The multi-inclusive community of faith was God's idea from the outset. Though the Hebrew people and, later, the early church, struggled to discern what that meant, the theme of inclusivity prevails in Scripture. Over time, Christianity transformed life in the Roman Empire. As the early Christians began to comprehend the thrust of Jesus' ministry, recognize his divinity, and connect his ministry to the work of God in the Hebrew Scriptures, there became a renewed awareness of what the original Abrahamic covenant was all about. It was this new and broad interpretation of the Old Testament, utilized in conjunction with the texts that would become the New Testament, that laid the foundation for a new type of religious community. This new type of community was what was so enticing initially and caused the church to grow so rapidly: "The central doctrines of Christianity prompted sustained attractive, liberating, and effective social relations and organization."[51] While this impetus has often been lost in contemporary Christianity, the basis for it remains. The church can still offer the hope and inspiration to become a liberating community of diversity, acceptance, and inclusivity, even though it won't be any easier now than it was then.

Without a doubt, "God's will for his creation is the establishment of a human society in which all the children enjoy perfect fellowship with each other, the created world, and the creator."[52] Accepting a clear biblical mandate for that purpose represents a start toward fulfilling God's will in the contemporary world. There remain other hurdles that must be overcome for this to be realized. The church must develop a theology of inclusivity based on the interpretation and application of the biblical mandate to progress. It must also be forthright in facing and addressing its tainted history of bigotry, genocide, enculturation, and exclusivity in order to make amends and work to establish a more inclusive theology, in line with God's will for the church.

FOR YOUR CONSIDERATION

Church Leader: In what ways have you been communicating the inclusive nature of God's love through the biblical story? In this hyperpoliticized and polarized cultural climate, it can be challenging to preach and teach this subject even if grounded in accepted orthodoxy and biblical interpretation. In what ways can support be obtained through other local pastors to work together on communicating this important message?

Sitting in the Pew: This understanding of Scripture may have broadened your understanding of how God chooses to work in the world. This chapter has been a very brief investigation into a theme that runs throughout Scripture. In what ways could you continue this investigation into the inclusiveness of God found in Scripture with others in your congregation/community?

Millennial/Gen Z: In what ways is this understanding of Scripture communicated consistently and clearly in your congregation? How could you involve yourself in discussing these things with other people in your community who may have different perspectives, particularly those from older generations?

All In: The interpretation of Scripture has always been a dynamic process, developing and changing according to the surrounding issues and culture. How might God working through this inclusive biblical understanding of God's intentions be a means of breaking down the polarizing barriers evident in society? Where in the wider community in which you live can you experience God's love for the variety of people found in humanity?

7

IT'S BIGGER THAN RACE
OR ETHNICITY

MUCH HAS BEEN WRITTEN recently regarding the Christian church and its issues of historical racism and ongoing racial bias. But there is more to it than simply the color of one's skin. There remains a cultural arrogance preventing people from diverse backgrounds from experiencing full participation and contributing to a broader understanding of God and a full expression of the family of God.

Separation and exclusion occur in many ways within a church setting. If one accepts the parish model described in an earlier chapter, it is probably easy to discern who from the parish is not adequately represented in each individual local congregation. What is it about our church that communicates to these outsiders that somehow they do not belong, at least not as they are? Exclusion from a church community occurs for a multitude of reasons, including ethnicity, culture, education level, socioeconomic standing, political bias, theology, ideology, and gender. Exclusivity is certainly bigger than just race or ethnicity, but we believe that the theological ideas that have permitted exclusivity on racial or ethnic grounds continue to permit exclusion for other reasons as well. Coming to terms with what has led the church to this point will require deep soul searching and a willingness to repent.

Inclusivity begins with accepting God's desire for the establishment of Christian community that reflects the breadth of God's love for all people. Stanley Grenz believes that ultimately,

"God's will for the creation is the establishment of a human society in which all children enjoy perfect fellowship with each other, the created world, and the creator."[1] This cannot happen in a context limited by discrimination and a misguided theology of assimilation that assumes the dominant social constructs should automatically be adopted by all.

A genuine multi-inclusive faith community is not simply one inhabited by people of various ethnicities and backgrounds who are then required to coalesce to the dominant culture. A genuine multi-inclusive community should reflect diversity in every aspect, including worship, communication, fellowship, and the leadership of the congregation. All participants should sense both that their cultural preferences are important and included but also that the cultural preferences of others with different identities are just as important and consistently included. Each participant should feel a level of comfort and familiarity as well as some discomfort and challenge.

This is difficult for any community, but particularly one that is attempting to transition from a monocultural to multi-inclusive congregation. As Mark DeYmaz states from his experience in leading a multiethnic congregation: "One critical outcome we have learned: in churches of living color, it will be a necessity to be comfortable with the uncomfortable. In other words, everyone involved has to defer at times to the preferences of others."[2] The willingness to accept discomfort for the greater good requires strong theological foundations, especially if churchgoers expect to find peace rather than challenge at church.

The willingness to experience discomfort to make the multiethnic and multi-inclusive church a reality is a challenge for most, particularly those who have held the power previously. The pandemic and racial unrest of 2020 is an example of that. In Northern California, I (Efrem) witnessed White brothers and sisters leave a predominantly White megachurch because the senior leaders wouldn't defy the state mandates from the governor and worship in the building. Once this church resumed meeting in their building but required the wearing of masks, that brought more anger from some. The senior pastor was accused of not having the courage to follow God above the governor.

I spoke to many pastors of these types of evangelical churches from across the country with similar Covid-19 state mandates, facing the same anger and threats to leave from some in their congregations. Often, members were only looking at the experience of Covid-19 from the perspective of how it was impacting predominantly White, suburban, and upper-class communities. In those communities, the number of people going to the hospital and the number of people dying were lower than in urban and predominantly Black and Brown communities. They assumed that the non-Whites in their church community or neighboring communities were experiencing it the same way. This perspective lacked cross-cultural awareness and empathy. Some had no willingness to explore how Covid-19 might have been impacting brothers and sisters and neighbors of color.

The racial unrest after the death of George Floyd was another moment where some within predominantly White evangelical churches resisted discomfort. In some of these churches, words like White privilege and systemic racism were quickly dismissed as socialism or reverse racism. Any exploration of the history and present reality of racial injustice was put under the banner of terms like critical race theory and "woke" theology. Uncomfortable conversations about race were met with charges of moving the church away from the gospel and giving into a liberal agenda that was antithetical to the Bible.

In my experience pastoring a multiethnic church, I have seen the response to discomfort around racial injustice differ from White brothers and sisters depending on their generation. Of course, this is not true in all cases, but many older White brothers and sisters get defensive and check out in these moments, while younger White brothers and sisters remain engaged. At Midtown Church, we lost some older Whites who just didn't have the spiritual and emotional capacity to hang in while their brothers and sisters of color shared their pain. One group of older White brothers and sisters in our church believed that the solution to the racialized pain that people of color were feeling was for them to admit that they were being deceived by liberal ideology and had internalized victimization.

This doesn't represent all older Whites in our church. There are older White brothers and sisters on our elder board, prayer team, and other leadership teams who have leaned in and been willing to navigate discomfort and join their brothers and sisters on the road of racial reconciliation and righteousness. And even more importantly they have been willing to follow Christ more deeply in navigating discomfort.

Jesus often made people uncomfortable. His very birth brought discomfort to political leaders. His declarations and demonstration of the good news and the kingdom of God brought discomfort to religious leaders. Some of his miracles drew large crowds and some of his messages led to a discomfort that drove people away. Then Jesus took on the incredible discomfort of physical beatings, incarceration, and the cross for our salvation. Reconciliation to God and one another through Christ is biblical. The apostle Paul is a significant advocate for and example of reconciliation in his call to bring the gospel to both the Jews and Gentiles. In 2 Corinthians 5, Paul writes about Christ followers being ambassadors of reconciliation.

One of the remaining roadblocks to developing the church into the multi-inclusive community God intended is its inherent ethnocentrism and the limited understanding of the impact this ideology has on individuals and communities. Even though one may believe that God loves people of all cultures and backgrounds, there frequently remains an assumption that God would best accomplish this work through one's own cultural constructs. The thinking goes that the language, liturgy, music, programs, and polity that have been most meaningful in our personal Christian experience is universally applicable to people of all cultures and walks of life. The result is that the predominant cultural ideology becomes that which is perceived as "normal" and therefore the one to which everyone should adhere. We introduced this idea in an earlier chapter using the term White normativity. This is clearly inhibiting the growth of the multi-inclusive church, preventing it from gaining full acceptance and limiting what is understood to be normal for the church as a whole.

While leadership might be cognizant of the fact that this narrow perspective of the Christian church will negatively impact the faith experience of those who do not share this dominant culture, it is difficult to relinquish the power that comes with it. Thus, the history of the Christian church, supported by Western, European ethnocentrism, continues to obstruct the viability of diverse faith communities.

For the most part, the church today is a segregated institution in an increasingly multiethnic world. Even in some churches with some diversity, the dominant group forces the other groups to assimilate into their culture, even if the dominant group (particularly Whites) is not fully aware that this is happening.[3]

In the contemporary church this may no longer be a conscious position promoted by people seeking to retain control, as might have been the case in the not-too-distant past. However, Terry Linhart believes much of what is currently happening within the church stems from a latent cultural ignorance, which stimulates a group of benevolent oppressors. These are usually very "compassionate people who end up harming [others] rather than helping."[4] In order to combat this benevolent oppression it becomes necessary to establish a strong theological platform for the multi-inclusive church, one that builds on the biblical foundations already discussed.

It is also vital to understand the historical context of race and culture within the institution of the church in the West. To simply dismiss this history as irrelevant events relegated to the past suggests that it has no ongoing influence on the contemporary church or society. For the church to move past its monoculturalism it must also accept that centuries of cultural subjugation and discrimination, as well as expectations of mandatory cultural assimilation, continue to shape the lives of ethnic minorities in the church and the wider culture.[5] There is no way to move the church into a new era of multiethnic community without first reconciling the mistakes of the past. It is therefore necessary to develop some understanding of the history of this ethnocentric ideology.

THE ISSUE OF RACE IN CONSIDERING A THEOLOGY FOR THE MULTI-INCLUSIVE CHURCH

Marcus Bell, a ministry director for Leader Up in Camden, New Jersey, and father to his own multiethnic family, believes that one of the issues preventing growth of diverse churches is that the Western Caucasian church is "unwilling to accept that it has been on the wrong side of history in many instances."[6] Instead of facing history humbly and penitently, churches all too often desire to forget and move on so as not to be disparaged by a past they believe they had no part in. However, this forgetting fails to address the issues or make any attempt at reconciliation or restitution.

Jamaal Williams, a leader of a multiethnic church in Louisville, Kentucky, shared with us some of the challenges of being an African American pastor in a formerly monocultural Caucasian church, one that specifically wanted to become multiethnic in line with its surrounding community. They lost hundreds of members as he began to address the difficult racial heritage of the US and Western church from the pulpit and promote worship styles associated with other cultures. He said he received constant communication that he had "forgotten the Gospel," "was transforming the church into a political

arena," and "was promoting socialist propaganda."[7] This demonstrates the effort by many parishioners in the majority to focus on
what they perceive to be the gospel, keeping what they believe to be
"political issues" out of the church. But these are often Western, Caucasian interpretations of what the gospel is all about.

There are many questions that need to be addressed. "How long
will the church in the West be able to reinvent itself when the majority of its people are no longer Western, European, or middle class?
The only way forward is to recenter the church to embrace the majority of the people who surround us."[8] Questions for those who
continue to retain control of church structure remain: "Why have
we taken up this space for so long? How can we repent and bring
restitution for having taken up so much space? How can we create
more space without feeling threatened by the presence of those not
previously accepted or included on their own terms?"[9]

Even pastors do not reflect the changing ethnic demographics of
the United States. Currently, of the more than thirty-one thousand
working pastors in the country, 73 percent are Caucasian, with just
over 10 percent African American and approximately 9 percent
Hispanic or Latino.[10] But as a nation, Caucasians represent only
58 percent of the general population, while the Hispanic population
is approximately 18 percent and the African American population
is currently 12 percent.[11] Within the next forty years, there will no
longer be an ethnic majority in the United States, but unless church
leadership begins to reflect those changes, it is likely that a significant portion of young people will not be able to see themselves in
a leadership role within a church or Christian organization. How are
they to believe that they have a place there?

With these demographic realities, not only is there a need for
seminaries, denominations, and church planting organizations to
focus on the crosscultural and intercultural development of White
pastors, but they also must invest in developing pastors from multiple backgrounds to plant and lead multiethnic and multi-inclusive

churches. This includes moving beyond presenting mostly White male leaders as the theological drivers of church planting and missional movements.

For too long, the role of presenting and interpreting Scripture has been unidirectional and almost universally seen as the responsibility of those self-designated as the authorities. But "placing biblical interpretation primarily in the hands of privileged people presents God's word in theologically myopic and often tyrannical ways."[12] The unspoken assumption has been that Western theology is the true theology and the interpretation best suited to understanding God and communicating the gospel.

But this belies the fact that the faith was founded in the East, and much of its early theology came from the African continent. The fear has been that syncretism will occur should other cultures be permitted to interpret the Scriptures from their own perspectives, discerning for themselves how best to express worship and what constitutes discipleship. According to Richard Twiss, a Native American Christian author, syncretism is

> seen as the consequence of combining good and evil, right and wrong, correct and false, biblical and heretical, godly and demonic, enlightened and deceived beliefs or practices resulting in falsehood, heresy, or ultimate deception. This cultural "deception" is identified by contrasting it to the theological standards of the "true" faith, which is firmly embedded in a Western polemic.[13]

Twiss believes that what is "at stake is the power to identify true religion and to authorize some practices as 'truthful' and others as 'false.'"[14] This lies substantially in the hands of Western European men. Relinquishing control of what is often considered Christian orthodoxy will not happen easily or even willingly. Yet, those growing up in more diverse contexts see this power struggle for what it is, and they continue to distance themselves from the Christian religion because of this evident hypocrisy. The silencing of other voices is anathema to them.

Some may dismiss the need for efforts to mold a more faithful theology as the foundation for the multi-inclusive church. It is easy to assume that since the current theology has been sufficient to sustain the church thus far, then little is to be gained by altering what exists. But theology has always been dynamic, not static. We continue to grow in our understanding of what God desires, and our theology is always shaped and influenced by our current circumstances. In this increasingly diverse social context, to refuse to grow our theology is to embrace irrelevance. Refusal to consider a theology that encourages diversity suggests that the monocultural model is what God intended. Yet, the biblical foundation and all the issues facing the church discussed thus far suggest otherwise. As culture and society change around the church, there must be renewed effort to interpret these circumstances theologically.

Miroslav Volf strongly argues for dynamic theology—the idea that as contexts change, so must Christian theology. He writes, "Theology ought to be about what matters the most—the true life in the presence of God . . . for theology is uniquely qualified to explore what matters the most and will either refocus itself on what matters the most or gradually cease to matter at all."[15] In this diversity, "Theology matters because it is about what matters the most for human life. Theology worth its name is about what we ought to desire above all things for ourselves and for the world."[16]

A theology of the inclusive church begins with the recognition that the racial and ideological tensions that divide communities are the result of a misguided social construct, and are not evident in the biblical record at all. As John Perkins reminds readers, "The term 'race' suggests more genetic categories among groups of human beings than is supported by scientific evidence."[17] Humanity's nature as the pinnacle of God's creation, according to the biblical record, was not compromised by any superficial or external category like skin tone, facial features, or the texture of one's hair. These categories were developed for the purposes of separation, subjugation, and maintaining dominance over others.[18] External markers continue to wield powerful influence on society, promoting a dualism of superiority and inferiority. The result is negative both for people of color and those claiming some nondescript form of White heritage.

According to Scripture there has only ever been one race, namely, the human race. The early Christians testified to this and sought to develop their faith beyond the historic boundaries of Hebrew culture and ethnicity. As they wrestled with the implications of God's universal love, they sought to communicate that God is the source and creator of humanity in its entirety, and therefore is to be realized as the Father of all.[19] Stanley Grenz notes that the early church believed themselves to be a unified "people called together by the proclamation of the Gospel for the purpose of belonging to God through Christ."[20] They developed an understanding of God's care as expansive, and the apostles' interpretation of the gospel of Jesus was central to this understanding.

The church grew to accept that only within a diverse community is the divine image realized.[21] David Smith points out that even within the church in Jerusalem, though universally the community was made up of Jews, "it was nonetheless socially and culturally pluralistic. From its very inception the Christian church was figuring out how to sustain fellowship amid differences of language and culture."[22] In practice this assumes that each congregation is meant to be the local expression of this unified church or family, the localized church of Jesus Christ. Therefore, "all the lofty phrases used in the New Testament regarding 'the church' are to be true of each congregation of believers."[23]

While no culture fully reflects the complete nature of God, each communicates unique aspects of God's image. Diverse community, then, is central to an inclusive theology and is critical to recognizing the church as the context where a more complete nature and image of God is evident. Full engagement with God can only occur in a diverse community, for it is "only in fellowship with others that we can show what God is like for God is the community of love."[24] This community of love can no longer be limited to those alike in most ways.

As a result of demographic forces in contemporary society, there is now an ever-growing cross section of diverse cultures evident throughout the world. Traditional, isolated cultural contexts no longer exist as distinctively as they once did. This reality has altered life for most people in numerous ways. As Mark Scandrette writes, "The organic kinship or household structures that were once the context for most people's lives have largely vanished. . . . The mobility and resulting fragmentation in our society requires us to become more conscious and intentional about sharing life together in the kingdom."[25] To be sure, Christians have long maintained an appreciation for God's love for the world and have sent missionaries to the farthest reaches to communicate that love. However, the need for crosscultural communication is no longer limited to those who feel called to leave their homeland and serve as missionaries. In most developed places around the globe, "the other side of the world may, in cultural terms, be just across the street. The chances of spending the rest of one's life solely in contact with people who are culturally alike are increasingly slim."[26]

This reality means that a special calling is no longer required for Christians to pursue relationships with those different from themselves. Diverse environments are the norm outside of most Christian congregations, particularly in the lives of young people. As a result, David Smith says, "Learning the dynamics of cultural difference can no longer be a special training restricted to missionaries. It is a necessary part of the learning that any disciple of Christ who desires to 'be a blessing' to those outside his or her immediate clan must undergo."[27]

The universal nature of the gospel is not limited to any specific cultural expression. Though individuals may experience the movement of God through a particular culture, such as eighteenth- or nineteenth-century European hymnody, contemporary Western worship music, or traditional Black gospel, God is not limited to these forms. If God is capable of communication through Western forms of expression, it is no less likely that other cultural expressions can result in the same powerful effect.[28] What this means is that in multi-inclusive faith communities, one should expect to experience a variety of expressions in worship and within other community gatherings. This will benefit all involved.

CHALLENGES TO MULTICULTURAL COMMUNITY

The desire to remain in monocultural Christian enclaves and to promote Western theology as normative stems from the historical influence of this branch of the church over many centuries. However, while Western European Christians still retain much of their previous power and influence, they can no longer be cast as representative of Christianity worldwide. In fact, according to David Smith, "the most striking feature of Christianity at the beginning of the third millennium is that it is predominantly a non-Western religion" and by 2050 only approximately one in five Christians will be non-Hispanic White.[29] As corporations, academic institutions, and social service organizations intentionally pursue diversity, somehow the church, which should have been at the forefront of this movement (especially in such a multiethnic context found in the developed world), continues to lag behind.

Even in seeking to fulfill the call to love and serve others as Jesus commands, there is a tendency to see service to others through the lens of the dominant culture. This generates the idea that anyone outside of the dominant group should be viewed as inherently poor, needy, and always requiring compassion. This permits the helper to retain their sense of superiority, even if it remains humbly expressed through compassionate acts.[30]

Much of this bias is rooted in implicit ethnocentric faith expressions in the West, which stem from the dark and rarely discussed history of racial bias in the Western church.[31] This history is largely unknown by many congregants, yet it continues to exert enormous negative influence on the contemporary church, prohibiting it in most instances from developing genuine diversity at all levels. Realizing and responding to this history and the ongoing influence it exerts is a critical component of pursuing genuine multi-inclusive worship communities.

Yet for more genuine expressions of diverse churches to develop, knowledge and confession must be the starting point. As C. S. Lewis testifies, a complete reversal must ensue. "A sum can be put right: but only by going back till you find the error and working it afresh from that point, never by simply going on. Evil can be undone, but it cannot 'develop' into good. Time does not heal it. The spell must be unwound, bit by bit."[32] In order for that spell to be unwound, recognition of its existence must be acknowledged, followed by overt and resolute steps to undo the wrongs, in order to become the church that God intended.

For a church to genuinely move toward becoming multi-inclusive, the dominant cultural group must be willing to permit the voices of others to be raised without fear of retribution or the expectation that they will soon need to acquiesce and assimilate to make everyone more comfortable. This generation, more than any other, recognizes that "the gospel dignifies every culture as a valid vehicle for God's revelation. Conversely, this also revitalizes every culture: no 'sacred' culture or language is the exclusive vehicle that God might use."[33]

However, multiple studies now indicate that a multicultural congregation only works as long as the Caucasians in the community remain comfortable.[34] Yet, to succeed, multi-inclusive churches "cannot be places where people of color [or those with any other differences] are expected to sacrifice who they are to belong, where they have to accommodate white people's predilections, comfort levels, and expectations for the sake of diversity."[35]

It is also insufficient to try to proceed by pretending that cultural differences do not exist. That stance also fails to acknowledge how God is found in variety and usually assumes once again that the dominant cultural force should prevail. "The danger in disregarding difference is that we risk creating a dominant, generic Christian monoculture, a one-size-fits-all model, while ignoring the complex tapestry of the community surrounding our local churches. There shouldn't be a prevailing Christian culture dictating church life in diverse environments."[36]

Neither is multi-inclusiveness permission to be "colorblind," as if that represents a means of overlooking difference. It doesn't dismiss the work that needs to be done on the three Rs of church ethnic relations: Repentance, Reconciliation, and Restitution. Multi-inclusivity is simply a means by which the church makes a great effort to reflect the entirety of the kingdom of God in all its facets.

Of all the likely challenges faced by a church seeking to become more inclusive, the issue of racial and cultural bias will almost certainly cause the most resistance. The metaphor of marriage can be a helpful way to understand what it means to truly embrace diversity. Mason Keiji Okubo describes this eloquently:

> Being married means having a relationship with another. It means incorporating that person into your life. It means considering their needs along with your own. It means being one flesh, sharing a life. It means intimacy. It means accepting differences. In fact, it means more than accepting. It means being able to fully understand the differences and celebrating them. As a result, the first years of marriage can be very tough,

because you are trying to learn to accommodate the lifestyles of another different human. To really be in a relationship is a lot of work. In the same way, being a [multi-inclusive] church is like being married.[37]

To learn to grow together, creating something completely new, where all contribute and grow together in faith different from anything any of them have known, is a beautiful image of what the church can become.

LEARNING FROM BLACK THEOLOGY, RECONCILIATION PRAXIS, AND URBAN APOLOGETICS

One of the ways to diversify the theological streams and ministry models that inform the multiethnic and multi-inclusive church is to stretch beyond the Western European and White exclusivity and normativity that currently exists. Some places to start in this stretching are Black theology, reconciliation praxis, and urban apologetics. For sure, Black theology and the history of the African American church has its own homogeneous and monocultural side. But pastors and theologians such as Howard Thurman, William Seymour, Martin Luther King Jr., John Perkins, James Cone, J. Deotis Roberts, Cheryl Sanders, and Brenda Salter McNeil have developed a theology and praxis of a multiracial, reconciling, and beloved community within Black theology and ministry praxis. African American Baptists, Evangelicals, and Pentecostals have been at the forefront of multiracial revivals, social movements, racial reconciliation initiatives, and multiethnic church planting. There are large multiethnic and multi-inclusive churches today led by African American pastors Albert Tate, Derwin Gray, Miles McPherson, Derrick Puckett, Leonce Crump, and myself (Efrem). There are multiethnic-church thought leaders such as Korie Edwards, Liz Rios (who is Afro-Latina), and Bryan Loritts. African Americans bring much to the table to strengthen the development of the multi-inclusive church.

The evangelical church especially can realize greater faithfulness and fruitfulness in the development of multiethnic and reconciling churches by learning from both the theology and the social engagement of the Black church. The civil rights movement is one example of a social engagement that was birthed out of the Black church but became an ecumenical and multiracial movement. This gift of Black liberation theology to the multiethnic and reconciling church is explored in the books *A Black Theology of Liberation* by James H. Cone and *A Black Political Theology* by J. Deotis Roberts. A third book, *Saints in Exile: The Holiness-Pentecostal Experience in African American Religion and Culture* by Cheryl J. Sanders, provides practical insight into how Black liberation theology and reconciliation praxis are realized in the life of the Black church and inform the development of multiracial congregations.

Cone's reflections on God in Black theology connect God as the liberator of the oppressed as seen in Exodus with the incarnational God found in Jesus Christ. This provides a union of both God the Father and God the Son as well as God the liberator and God the reconciler.[38] Meanwhile, Roberts presents a Black theology that calls the oppressed to the pursuit of both liberation and reconciliation based not on cheap grace, but on a faith in the God who suffers with the marginalized and sets them free. This also points to the incarnational God found in Jesus Christ as he encounters the oppressed, marginalized, and suffering. This combination of liberation and reconciliation empowers the oppressed to set the terms to the oppressors on which reconciliation to God and one another are possible.[39] Sanders explores the journey of Third Street Church of God in Washington, DC, as a church of refuge and reconciliation. This ministry of being a refuge from a world of sin and a house of reconciliation to divided humanity puts into practice the theological union of liberation and reconciliation. It also informs how a multiethnic and reconciling church can put the learnings from Black theology and the journey of the Black church into its outreach and discipleship initiatives.[40]

The journey of the Black church and Black preachers in the United States has included both a Black liberation and reconciliation praxis. Being reconciled to God through Christ, the liberation of Black people in an oppressed society, and ministries attempting racial reconciliation have all been part of this journey for a people who began as slaves. Pastor and theologian Cheryl Sanders explores part of this journey of the Black church and Black preachers in her book *Saints in Exile: The Holiness-Pentecostal Experience in African American Religion and Culture.* Her presentation of the development of interracial movements within the African American Holiness-Pentecostal journey partially informs the ministry praxis of the reconciling church. Sanders provides a brief background sketch of the five original denominations coming out of the Holiness-Pentecostal movement and the impact of racism on them. Three out of the five denominations were interracial on some level, but they were deeply impacted by racism from Whites within the denomination or the pressure of White racism from the outside.[41]

This brief sketch by Sanders shows a historic openness and commitment to racial reconciliation by Blacks with Whites while still being subjugated to racism by them. What a powerful commitment to reconciliation on the part of the Black participants! Black people historically are at the forefront of the reconciling church while simultaneously working to realize their own liberation. In the early 1900s, Blacks and Whites in the Holiness-Pentecostal movement worked together to plant churches, but probably at a greater cost to the Black brothers and sisters. The Azusa Street Revival is an example of a multiracial and reconciling event, led by African American apostle William J. Seymour. However, Sanders states that Seymour was not alone in making the Azusa Street Revival and the Azusa Street Mission a success:

Although the Azusa Street Mission attracted a multiracial multitude of black, white, Hispanic, Native American, and Asian seekers of both sexes and all social classes, the fact remains that its fundamental identity as a group of poor black women and men significantly facilitated the revival's broad appeal.[42]

This is important to the development of the reconciling church because it is a reminder of the way in which reconciliation takes place through the incarnation of God in Christ. Reconciliation is made possible in Christ spiritually, but there is a unique way in which this spiritual event has social significance. Christ does not come as a wealthy, privileged Roman with his ministry of liberation and reconciliation. God reveals himself in Christ as a marginalized, oppressed minority born in an impoverished condition. Yet from this state of being, reconciliation is possible.

Connect this now to marginalized and oppressed Black people within the Holiness-Pentecostal movement participating in ministries of reconciliation. Who Christ is and how he came in human form are significant for how the church becomes a reconciling movement. The journey of the Black church and the Black struggle for liberation and openness to reconciliation can better inform the mission of the reconciling church than that of Western European theology and the ministry praxis of White evangelicalism.

Reconciliation theology and praxis can also strengthen the multi-inclusive church. This is an obvious place to start because within reconciliation theology and praxis there are African American theologians and practitioners who have laid the foundation on which to plant and develop multiethnic and reconciling churches.

It is important here to define a reconciling church. In her book *Roadmap to Reconciliation*, Dr. Brenda Salter McNeil defines the term reconciliation as "an ongoing spiritual process involving forgiveness, repentance and justice that restores broken relationships and systems to reflect God's original intention for all creation to flourish."[43] With this definition in mind, a reconciling church is one that embraces the ongoing spiritual process that involves forgiveness, repentance, and a justice that restores broken relationships and systems, and weaves it into its discipleship strategies. The reconciling church is justice oriented and equips Christians to be disciple makers in an ethnically diverse and deeply divided mission field. For this ecclesiastical practice of reconciliation to take place externally, it must first show up internally among an ethnically diverse staff and volunteer leadership within the church.

Salter McNeil's book is a major contribution to the development of reconciliation theology. She provides the necessary framework for moving reconciliation beyond simply a social experiment or relational tool to a weapon of spiritual warfare, the primary mission of the church and one of the fundamental elements of spiritual development. She even places the beginnings of reconciliation theology much earlier than the development of multiethnic churches or the writings of the apostle Paul on reconciliation in the New Testament. Though reconciliation is the restorative and repairing work of God in Christ and God's people through the church, Salter McNeil roots reconciliation theology in the Genesis account of the Garden of Eden and provides a broader understanding of what broken humanity is being restored back to. She presents this understanding of multiethnic diversity being the mission of God in the beginning of creation in the following manner:

> So, let's press into our theology of reconciliation. It starts in Genesis 1:28 with what is known as "the cultural mandate," or the command to fill the earth. Here we see that variation was one of God's creational motives from the outset. The creation account reveals God's desire for the earth to be filled with a great diversity of races and people.[44]

Though we have argued that race is a non-biblical and manmade social construct, we agree with her overarching point: both oneness and diversity were God's ideas from the beginning. God commanded the first human beings to move toward the reality of a flourishing, multiplying, unified diversity in relationship with God and one another. Sin warps this idea and creates separation between God and humanity; it also impacts God's vision of a diverse humanity. The diversity of humanity infected by sin leads to division and oppression. Christ as the ultimate reconciler comes to restore human beings and the rest of creation back to God's original vision. This provides a more robust reconciliation theology for the multiethnic church. The multiethnic church is a flourishing church of justice and transformation when adopting a reconciliation theology and strategy for developing a culture of reconciliation.

Salter McNeil then moves in her book to presenting a reconciliation praxis, which she calls a "roadmap." She believes that racialized events, even the most tragic ones, can be used by the church as catalysts to the process of reconciliation. She provides two potential options that can take place within a catalytic event: people will either seek preservation or desire transformation. Preservation is a defense option for staying with the racial or ideological beliefs that one already holds. In this option, a person digs his or her heels deeper in the ground. For example, a White person choosing to preserve his or her whiteness as it is regardless of how it is impacting people of color. Another example would be a male choosing to preserve his overt masculinity as it is currently, even if this is at the expense of sustaining an oppressive or unsafe environment for women.

Transformation is the option Salter McNeil provides for those who desire to step into the process of reconciliation. Her roadmap includes an invitation to journey into repentance, justice, and forgiveness. This roadmap is very useful because many people are coming into the multiethnic church deeply impacted by a culture infected by rampant preservationism, especially in the areas of race and political ideology. Because of this, it is possible for a person to experience spiritual transformation through the receiving of Christ as Lord and Savior and yet stay in preservation mode socially or culturally. However, spiritual transformation as reconciliation ought to bring about an ongoing holistic transformation. For the apostle Paul, for instance, his meeting Christ on the road to Damascus brought about an internal spiritual transformation and it also brought about a social transformation in how he saw and related to both Jewish and Gentile followers of Christ. He is so spiritually and socially transformed that he praises God even in persecution, and he influences the planting of multicultural and reconciling churches that pursue justice. The reconciling church is an embassy of this holistic reconciliation and transformation. Salter McNeil's roadmap provides a way to frame and measure this.

The reconciling church also focuses externally on its surrounding mission field. The late Reverend Samuel Hines described reconciliation as both a spiritual discipline and the primary agenda of the church.[45] Understanding the reconciling church in this way shows a dynamic relevancy for greater participation and fruitfulness in the Great Commission in urban America and beyond. Since the Great Commission is about making disciples of all nations, in America, this is a crosscultural, social justice, and reconciling venture. There is no significant fulfilling of the Great Commission without acknowledging and addressing racial injustice, racism, and the challenge of whiteness and white supremacy within the evangelical church and beyond.

Urban apologetics, which is fairly new as a more formal stream of Christian theology, is useful as well for the development of multi-inclusive churches. Urban apologetics is a theology for the city and from the margins. Some expressions of urban apologetics are more of a Black apologetics addressing the opportunity to be missional within a growing Black humanism and other religious and spiritual movements within African American culture such as the Nation of Islam, Five Percenters, and Hebrew Israelites. Another segment of urban apologetics is about the embodiment of the gospel within the broader and more multicultural landscape that is the city. Cities are the most visible picture of multiculturalism and more progressive ideologies. Cities are also the most visible picture of racial disparities. In cities, many social challenges cannot be avoided.

Some helpful book resources on urban apologetics include *Urban Apologetics: Why the Gospel is Good News for the City* by Christopher W. Brooks, *The Woke Church: An Urgent Call for Christians in America to Confront Racism and Injustice* by Eric Mason, and *From Classism to Community: A Challenge for the Church* by Jini Kilgore Cockroft. Urban apologetics informs the ministry praxis of the multiethnic and reconciling church by presenting a practical theology of the priesthood of all believers (1 Peter 2:9-10) through the embodiment of the good news, which is the gospel of Christ (Luke 4:18-21). In this way the church becomes the continuing extension of the incarnation of God as ambassadors of reconciliation, until Christ returns (2 Corinthians 5:14-21).

Brooks presents the members of the urban church as urban apologists, whose lives show how much the city and its challenges matter to God. Urban apologists embody the gospel in ways that show how Christ and the gospel have much to say about social issues. He contends that the mission of the urban church is to present a Christianity that is concerned with the human flourishing of those historically and currently marginalized and oppressed.[46] Because urban centers are ripe for the development of multiethnic and reconciling churches, this understanding of urban apologists can inform the development of justice-oriented disciple makers.

Mason presents the members of the urban church as exiles and as incarnational missionaries for justice. In his defining of incarnational missionaries for justice, he shows how peacemaking, justice, and image bearing are crucial elements of the missional and urban church. When urban Christians find identity in being incarnational missionaries for justice, they become woke Christians and collectively a woke church.[47] Becoming "woke" is a useful metaphor in the moving from a Christian who is a member of a diverse church to one who steps into the journey of justice-oriented disciple making.

Kilgore Cockroft contends that followers of Christ in community together should lead to a fellowship of equals, where racial and social class lines are dismantled. Her vision for the urban church goes beyond simply being together in a diverse community to how people treat one another, learn from each other, and grow spiritually in such an environment. For her, an urban and diverse congregation ought to bring about a deeper spiritual transformation and realization of extended family among the haves and the have-nots and, for instance, the formally incarcerated and never incarcerated.[48]

WHAT NOW?

The church in the West is engulfed in an ocean of distortions and deceptions that in large part continue to prevent it from becoming what the world needs and what God ordained it to be.[49] If ignored or glossed over, the church's racial and ethnic history will only maintain the status quo and leave the church encumbered by it. Further, as emerging generations continue to become more comfortable with diversity, they'll see the monocultural church as antiquated, bigoted, and disinterested in genuine forms of justice and equality. The monocultural church also communicates assimilationist tendencies, which explain much of the reticence for involvement by most of those considered ethnic minorities.

Here is the message for the church, not only in the past but also for the present. As it struggles with its historical involvement in the development of the racialized and polarized society in which it is engulfed and admits its continuing silent complicity in the ongoing systemic injustices, it must also realize that those tendencies do not simply disappear. Volf makes this clear. "In many diverse situations, the temptation to falsify God's word, to spin it to say what people want it to say—or what theologians themselves want it to say—can

be strong."[50] This is frequently done by dismissing historic cata-
strophic and racially motivated subjugation of minorities as echoes
of the past, deemed no longer relevant in the contemporary world
or church. But to move toward inclusivity, these events cannot be
dismissed simply because Caucasian Christians are embarrassed by
them. "Just as we cannot take out the parts of the Bible that we don't
like or that make us uncomfortable, we can't celebrate the shining
moments of the Western church's history and then ignore the
shameful aspects of that history."[51] This is what C. S. Lewis expresses
so clearly in his example of fixing a mathematical mistake or a
wrong turn. This history needs to be addressed and dealt with
openly and forthrightly for the church to be restored to its diverse
and inclusive first-century roots.

The long-term impact on the church has been blindness to the
experience of others and an embracing of privilege even when that
privilege is denied. "Whites [have] acted in a superior manner for so
long that it [is] difficult for them to even recognize their cultural and
spiritual arrogance."[52] The result is that the eyes of the culturally
dominant interpret Scripture and the events in the early church
from this dominant perspective instead of recognizing the inclusivity and multiculturalism that was evident at the foundation of
Christianity.[53] This, then, becomes the interpretation that has been
used to suppress those from different cultures deemed inferior. Even
now, in contemporary society, it propagates assimilationist tendencies toward diverse cultures and any brave individuals willing to
risk participating in a multicultural faith community.

This cannot continue to be the position of the church. Emerging
generations will not tolerate a segregated church. The biblical
mandate clearly indicates that God's desire is for a diverse community of believers so that Christians may have greater experience
of the *imago Dei*, "image of God." There is a strong theology available
to help move the church toward fulfillment of this hope.

FOR YOUR CONSIDERATION

Church Leader: People rarely appreciate discomfort, especially in a church context. Yet, to become the multi-inclusive church a broader theology must be developed. Forcing people of different backgrounds, ethnicities, and the like to assimilate to your cultural context will continue to erect barriers to their inclusion. What are the theological threads most needed in your context? Where can you find help to broaden your own understanding and perspectives? In what ways can you communicate the difficult history of the Caucasian church and begin the process of reconciliation?

Sitting in the Pew: To become a more inclusive congregation, we need to accept that others don't worship or practice their faith in the same way that we do. What are the aspects of your faith experience that you hold most dear (worship style, music, liturgy) that others may not practice in the same way? What might a blended community look like? How might experiencing other preferences for worship and liturgy help you grow in your faith and understanding of God?

Millennial/Gen Z: What different types of worship and faith communities have you had the opportunity to experience? Has this been helpful in broadening your understanding of who God is and how others' experiences of God differ from your own? In what ways do you think it might be helpful to share your experiences with more traditional members of your congregation? What are some places where you could invite them to share some of the experiences you have had?

All In: Becoming a multi-inclusive faith community will be an arduous process of growth and development. All within the congregation will face periods of discomfort and challenge at times. Accepting the difficult racial history of the church is not a political perspective, but one necessary for reconciliation and full inclusion of people of diverse backgrounds. Holding on to our personal preferences loosely will allow us to experience new and different experiences. What in this possibility are you anxious about? Excited about?

8

TOWARD BECOMING A
MULTI-INCLUSIVE CONGREGATION

MY (DAN'S) HEART FOR SEEING the worldwide church become
the multi-inclusive community I believe God desires began to develop as I met young people at various youth events, conferences, and
within the college where I was teaching. I repeatedly heard their frus-
trations with what they felt their church represented. They were
struggling with many of the issues defined by Hailey in the introduction to this book. They had a sense that the doors of the church
were closed to many of their friends—perhaps not literally, but barriers were present in the disparity between the love of Jesus they were
learning about and the way they felt the church communicated that
love to those different from themselves.

I realized that in my home church at the time, in East Tennessee,
we could never become a multiethnic church based on our surrounding demographics. But we were monocultural beyond simply
ethnicity. There was a specific socioeconomic, educational, ideological, and political bent to our congregation that largely did not
reflect the surrounding community. We all have a natural inclination
to gather with people like us, but this inclination limits us in many
ways, especially in living as vibrant members of the family of God.

Traveling, observing, interviewing, reading, and researching led
me to understand that churches often communicated unspoken and
unintentional messages about who was "in" and who was "out."
These were counter to what is consistently promoted in Scripture.

Some churches were therefore missing out on a fuller, deeper, broader experience of God as a result. Clearly, in Christ we are one family, and the church is meant to be a tapestry—so much more dynamic when it is vibrant. While we understand this intellectually, it is challenging to implement.

Each congregation will need to discern for themselves how to embrace the concept of multi-inclusivity and begin the work toward its realization within their community. This work will have to include coming to terms with ideas of difference and otherness. It will require giving current congregants opportunities to share the realizations they are coming to and the growth they are undergoing. It will also mean holding personal preferences regarding worship and other corporate experiences more loosely than they might have in the past. Each congregation will need to develop their own approach, fulfilling God's specific mission for their place in the world. Ultimately, we agree with Dwight Zsheile that "the church as the body of Christ thrives when it, too, dwells deeply within its surrounding communities, joining neighbors there."[1] A thriving church does not necessarily mean a large church, but it does anticipate that stronger connections will be built with those who have been outsiders, namely emerging generations and those from other cultures and backgrounds.

The pandemic changed the scorecard for the church. The shutdown caused by Covid-19 incited a reevaluation of what the church represents as well as how, and why, people remain involved. Most churches have still not returned to 2019 involvement numbers, and measures of success such as attendance, buildings, and annual budget will likely not be the metrics of the future. The faithfulness and fruitfulness of the church moving forward will be based on the impact and influence it has in an ever-increasing multicultural, multiethnic, metropolitan, and polarized mission field. Urbanization is having a tremendous impact on the mission field of much of the West. In many places, suburbs are looking more like cities and rural areas are looking more like suburbs. Homogeneous churches are experiencing greater ethnic, racial, and economic class diversity in their surrounding communities.

A new missional opportunity calls for the planting and development of multi-inclusive churches that will reproduce themselves. Current multiethnic and reconciling churches must develop a passion and strategy for multiplication and reproduction. Most models of multiplication and reproduction are based on large, predominantly White, multicampus churches. Many of those models are based on a lone White male preacher being pumped into the other campuses of the church through video streaming. This assumes that the primary-campus church, typically in a predominantly White suburb, is missionally relevant to the multicultural and metropolitan landscape. There is a need to imagine the Christian community based on a heavenly vision and a passion to reach a multicultural mission field. Again, Revelation 7:9 comes to mind as the biblical foundation for this reimagining of the church: "After this I looked, and there before me was a great multitude that no one could count, from every nation, tribe, people and language, standing before the throne and before the Lamb. They were wearing white robes and were holding palm branches in their hands."

With the nation being deeply polarized by politics and socially suffocating from racial injustice, we must ask what evangelistic, disciple making, and missional credibility the church has, even a diverse church. The development of the multi-inclusive church alone is not enough to bring transformation to a diverse, divided, and polarizing mission field. Will the development of crosscultural and justice-oriented disciple makers in a multiethnic congregation increase the credibility and relevancy of churches located in an ever-increasing metropolitan and multicultural context? Can these existing and reproducing multi-inclusive churches advance racial reconciliation and righteousness in the midst of racial injustice and unrest? And can these churches reach and provide refuge for the emerging generations so that they would be empowered to reengage their world as reconcilers? Multi-inclusive churches are the best environment to equip and release crosscultural and justice-oriented disciple makers who forge unity, transformation, and social justice in their local communities. These are the needed reconcilers who can innovate new paths of evangelism and missions.

Viewing a church's geographical setting as a parish provides a better means of measuring growth in the area of diversity and inclusivity. Within the parameters established for the parish lie all the different pieces of the mosaic, or the possible contents of the salad bowl, ready to be included to bring God's creation in the church to its full potential. This encourages the church to look beyond numbers and instead address barriers to exclusion. It also focuses attention outside the walls of the church building itself, recognizing that the care of souls within the parish is not bound by walls, attendance, programs, or traditions. It broadens responsibility for the change beyond church staff, recognizing each congregant as a minister of the gospel.

Claiming the surrounding community as a parish also provides the opportunity toward a more inclusive church, because it prompts a reimagining of culture. Churches generally take one of two views in their relationship to culture. For some parts of the church, culture is seen as the enemy, being defined as "the world" against which Christians are at war. It is therefore not entered with compassion and grace as a mission field. Seeing culture as the enemy limits our ability to more fully live into the Great Commission and the call to serve as ambassadors of reconciliation.

But another segment of the church takes a different approach to culture. Instead of the culture being an enemy, it is embraced. The surrounding community dictates the DNA and mission of these churches. This can happen in both conservative and liberal churches; these churches are liberal or conservative because of the surrounding community. If the church is in a conservative area, the church represents that cultural and ideological reality. If the surrounding community is liberal, the church represents that cultural and ideological reality. Some churches have changed their position on social issues based on the changing demographics within their surrounding community, not a truly deep revelation from the Scriptures.

We are suggesting a different approach, which neither sees culture as the enemy nor fully embraces its beliefs and values. Both of these approaches lead to religious arrogance and idolatry. Instead, we suggest a missional engagement with culture that views it with compassion, empathy, love, and a biblical justice orientation.

For those who see the community as the enemy, this means moving away from judging people within the culture to journeying with people in the culture. It means having the type of spiritual transformation that the apostle Paul had with Christ followers. He goes from persecuting Christians to becoming one of them. He goes from judging people who didn't believe like him to journeying with them. He went from judging them for death to pursuing them for new life (Acts 22:1-21; Galatians 1:11-21). Of course, when it comes to reaching those who don't know Christ, this isn't an apples-to-apples example, but the fruit of Paul's transformed heart is what we learn from. Even when speaking to pagans, he engages the culture by learning about their worship, arts, and political beliefs; he uses their own poets to share the good news of Jesus Christ with them (Acts 17:16-32). Paul's transformed heart led to a new social engagement and spiritual agenda.

One example of this tension is the Black Lives Matter movement. When Midtown Church was a campus of a larger evangelical multi-campus church, some members wanted us to make a statement against Black Lives Matter. There were many others in the church who didn't feel the same way. The former group, mostly if not exclusively White, wanted us to also pass a policy that church staff couldn't use the hashtag #BlackLivesMatter on social media. Others wanted us to talk about the Black Lives Matter organization as being antithetical to the Bible. There were two problems here. One, the people who wanted the church to do these things didn't live in proximity to people who identified with the Black Lives Matter movement. They didn't know their names or stories. All their views came from what they saw on the news and what they read on websites, not relationships.

This group also wanted to bless and minister to police officers. There were discussions about putting on a marriage retreat for police officers and their spouses. Law enforcement and other public servants were honored within the weekend worship services of the suburban campuses. But there was no discussion of putting on marriage retreats for community activists and their spouses. There was no discussion about the prioritizing of ministry initiatives for those who identified with Black Lives Matter. In this moment, the social and cultural expressions coming out of the Black Lives Matter movement had become the enemy for many, while the social and cultural expressions coming out of law enforcement were being fully embraced. This was part of a larger reality in which liberal political ideology and social justice movements were seen as the enemy of evangelicalism, while conservative political ideology was fully embraced. But this dissecting of culture hinders the broader evangelistic and disciple-making potential of the church. In this approach, the church divides those within their surrounding metropolitan mission field into the categories of friends and enemies.

When we were part of this larger church, our campus was the only urban and center-city campus. Uniquely, our Midtown campus had proximity to those who identified with the Black Lives Matter movement locally in Sacramento. They were part of our church; we knew them by name, and we knew their stories. They were part of our surrounding community. So, to make a statement against Black Lives Matter and to make them our enemy in some way would deeply impact our missional credibility. But we had police officers attending our church as well. We knew their names, their families, and their stories too. Our desire as a campus was to engage the lives of both those who identified with expressions of the Black Lives Matter movement and police officers—because they both made up the diverse community in which our campus is located. If we truly wanted to be a multi-inclusive church, we couldn't afford to make friends out of some members of our community and enemies out of others. We wanted a broader missional reach within the city of Sacramento.

This is one of the reasons our church transitioned from being a campus of a large, multicampus, mostly suburban and White church to going on our own and becoming Midtown Church: a metropolitan, multiethnic, multi-inclusive, and multicampus church. Becoming a multi-inclusive church will require courageous and tough decisions. It will cause discomfort and, in some cases, pain. In making the decision to become a multi-inclusive church, you may lose people who came to the church with no desire to be challenged around their political ideologies versus being transformed toward a larger kingdom vision of multiethnicity and multi-inclusivity. But the journey of Midtown Church in Sacramento is just one way toward becoming a multi-inclusive church; it's not the only way.

My (Dan's) story is different from what Efrem went through in Sacramento. I pastor a traditional, mainline church in a suburban area of Atlanta. Though Atlanta is a diverse metropolitan community, much of that diversity is not found north of the city, where our church is located. As much as it pains me to say, our congregation is not very diverse. So, during the racial unrest of 2020, many in our congregation expressed similar sentiments as those described by Efrem: a belief that society was in meltdown and things should be done to ensure that this rhetoric did not infiltrate our community. However, our leadership felt that what was happening provided an opportunity to help shift the narrative for many in our church.

Initially, we formed groups to read and discuss important books that would provide context and understanding for the evident unrest. These texts included *The Color of Compromise* by Jemar Tisby, *I'm Still Here* by Austin Channing Brown, *Be the Bridge* by Latasha Morrison, and *Reconstructing the Gospel* by Jonathan Wilson-Hartgrove. This was difficult work and led to deep and challenging discussions— with multiple angry emails from members who felt that "woke" theology had taken over. Several of our pastors joined protests calling for justice and the recognition that Black lives do matter, asking those they were leading in these studies to join them.

In addition, the church became more intentional about connecting with traditional African American churches in our immediate vicinity. We made efforts to join them in outreach and justice initiatives. Our role was simply to demonstrate solidarity and to be directed by the vision of people whose life and experience are different from our own. We have fostered relationships across ethnic lines that were rarely crossed before.

I would hardly call this a success story, or even a significant move toward becoming a multi-inclusive church. But, for those who participate there has been growth, a willingness to admit bias and bigotry, and a recognition that reconciliation is their responsibility. We have even seen evidence of some from emerging generations who had not darkened the door of the church since they were in the youth group showing up to participate alongside brothers and sisters from the African American churches to serve in the community. Some evidence, though small, that these actions provide them a chance to be the church instead of just going to church.

These stories and the examples of churches working to broaden their reach provided in chapter three demonstrate that there is no perfect way to become multi-inclusive. Each congregation will need to do their own soul searching, be vigilant in prayer, observe their own community, and find their ways to serve. It will require some open discussions from elders or the wider congregation about the desire to remove barriers of inclusion and the possible implications of this transformation. Open and honest discussions will be critical.

The objective is not to disrupt current modes of being simply to try something new, but to foster growth within the community and as individuals.

STEPS IN THE PROCESS OF BECOMING MULTI-INCLUSIVE

Some tools may be useful in beginning the process. The first step will be to discern the demographics of the congregation as it currently exists, including gender, ages, marital status, estimated socioeconomic status, education levels, ethnicity, distance they travel for worship, and any other aspects that seem relevant. Once this is done, it should not be difficult to find information about city or county demographics to compare to the congregation. That provides a starting point for determining how well the congregation reflects the surrounding community. The next step is discerning the gaps, the needs that can be served there, and what resources are currently available to begin to meet those needs. This encourages the church to be a force for good within the community, providing unconditional love and service.

There are other things to consider when preparing a congregation for greater inclusiveness that will alert them to their own hidden and unrecognized biases. Practical measures should include developing purposeful connection with other congregations in the community, particularly those with a different ethnic or social makeup. The intent of these connections is not to attempt a merge, but to express the unity found in the body of Christ and to begin working together to create a more holistic and inclusive Christian community. These connections need to be greater than simply a monthly meeting of ministry leaders. Opportunities for pulpit exchanges, joint community service projects, celebrations, and social occasions will over time create a greater sense of unity and camaraderie rather than a spirit of competition.

This has been the main impetus for the church I now serve in the greater Atlanta area. We are trying to be intentional about creating opportunities for our congregants to serve in our immediate area with our neighbor churches, which are strong African American congregations. Careful not to dictate the terms, we have posted opportunities for our members to come alongside projects initiated by their leadership. This has led to collaborative community engagement and opportunities for all involved to establish meaningful crosscultural relationships. We have also opened our facilities for use with local nonprofit agencies that care for people who are housing or food insecure. We seek to serve these ministries on their terms and provide support to ensure that those they serve are welcomed and supported not as outsiders but as others on the journey toward wholeness like everyone else. These opportunities have provided further chances for volunteers to know and serve people in our community.

Efforts similar to this can be made toward intentional diversification of social networks of parishioners where possible. This may not be possible within a congregation lacking much diversity. Thus, the engagement with other congregations may offer opportunity for this development. Short-term combined small groups or intentional mixing of congregations for community service projects will help diversify an individual's social contacts necessary to develop greater understanding. While this may cause some discomfort and even potential refusal from some people it is imperative if the church is to be integral to the reduction of the polarization evident in society.

When I (Efrem) was serving as a pastor in Minneapolis, Minnesota, I was part of the development of two networks that brought congregations together and informed a greater inclusivity within churches. One was a network of youth pastors called Urban RECLAIM. Our vision was to missionally reclaim our city, specifically its young people. This reclaiming of young people was about joining God in believing that young people had the gifts and abilities to serve as young heroes for God in their own communities. Through the reclaiming of God's vision for young people from the

Scriptures, youth themselves could bring about transformation through the church in the Twin Cities.

This network brought youth pastors together across the Twin Cities of Minneapolis and Saint Paul. There were both youth pastors from within local congregations as well as from parachurch organizations such as Young Life, Youth for Christ, and Cru. We met monthly to encourage each other and learn from one another. We put on outreach events together and youth leader retreats. There were local churches whose reach into their surrounding community was strengthened through these efforts. Deeper relationships were built between local churches and parachurch ministries. I was one of the core leaders of this network when I was a youth pastor at Park Avenue United Methodist Church in southern Minneapolis from the years 1999 to 2003. Park Avenue was one of the largest multi-ethnic and multi-inclusive churches in the Twin Cities at the time.

A second network was called Bridges of Reconciliation. This was a network of Senior Pastors and city movement leaders across the Twin Cities of Minneapolis and Saint Paul. It was mostly made up of pastors of predominantly White suburban churches and predominantly Black urban churches. But the network came about through the planting of Sanctuary Covenant Church, a multi-ethnic and multi-inclusive church in northern Minneapolis in 2003. I was privileged to be the church planter of Sanctuary Covenant Church with my wife, Donecia. Our church plant was supported by the Evangelical Covenant Church denomination, but also received support from three large predominantly White suburban churches and two very influential urban African American churches. Significantly, these churches didn't simply want to give financial and people resources to the planting of Sanctuary Covenant Church, they wanted to stay in relationship as pastors and churches believing this would lead to a larger kingdom impact in the Twin Cities.

From this relational and missional desire came the development
of Bridges of Reconciliation, a network committed to racial reconciliation and righteousness and transformational missional initiatives. Like Urban RECLAIM, pastors met monthly for encouragement and the strengthening of our churches through peer
mentoring. We had pulpit exchanges as well as worship team and
choir exchanges between our churches. We put on a citywide
worship experience called Kingdom in the City. Some of the predominantly White suburban churches launched initiatives and
put on forums that led to their churches becoming more diverse
and inclusive. Some of the predominantly Black urban churches
made a commitment for the first time to develop youth and young
adult ministries, including hiring younger pastors to oversee them.
Models of both multiethnic and intergenerational inclusive ministries were launched in churches through the network of Bridges
of Reconciliation.

When I became colead pastor of what is now Midtown Church
of Sacramento in 2017, I was blessed to get connected to a network
called City Pastors Fellowship of Sacramento (CPF), led by Pastors
Don and Christa Proctor. As soon as I was called to Midtown
Church as colead pastor, I received an invitation to a luncheon put
on by CPF to welcome me and my wife to Sacramento. At the
luncheon, we were welcomed by an ethnically diverse group of
pastors and spouses. We were given gifts and told that there was
no competition between pastors and churches in the Sacramento
region, but a desire to fellowship and grow together as a larger
kingdom family.

I was blown away by this—a group of pastors in a new city welcoming us warmly, inviting us to participate in ministering alongside
them with complete trust and no sense of competition. My first year
in Sacramento I had almost weekly invitations to have breakfast,
coffee, or lunch with a pastor in the Sacramento region. I was invited
to preach in other churches and built genuine friendships with other

pastors. CPF puts on quarterly fellowship luncheons for pastors and spouses, encourages pulpit exchanges, has a NextGen initiative for youth and young adult pastors, and sponsors an annual citywide Martin Luther King Jr. service. The development of networks is one way to strengthen churches toward multi-inclusivity.

There are some other tools to consider as efforts are made to engage the community at large. The Fuller Youth Institute, in their book *Growing Young,* describes six core commitments churches must apply to "grow young," or connect with emerging generations.[2]

1. Unlock keychain leadership
2. Empathize with today's young people
3. Take Jesus' message seriously
4. Fuel a warm community
5. Prioritize young people (and families) everywhere
6. Be the best neighbors[3]

Clearly, these commitments overlap with the strategies necessary for churches to become diverse and inclusive. The focus on keychain leadership, being clear about the message of Jesus (which would include the interpretations that people of other cultures have of him), fostering a warm and inclusive community, and becoming the best neighbors all serve to strengthen both the multigenerational and multi-inclusive dimensions of any congregation.

Some may be concerned that it is too late for their congregation, or that their church is not "cool" enough to connect meaningfully. However, the commitments defined by Fuller Youth Institute do not necessarily require churches to change denominations, worship or preaching styles, architecture, or furniture to become multi-inclusive. Nevertheless, they will require churches to make some purposeful investment (not necessarily financial), and be intentional about developing a long-term strategy toward becoming young and reflecting the demographics of their surrounding community.

Once a congregation embraces a parish model of ministry, the aim becomes a vision toward full immersion within local communities. In this way the church is more likely to thrive, though it should be clear that this does not mean that it will grow numerically. There will be a need to develop new metrics of success for congregations willing to look beyond numbers to other measures for determining success as a church. But as Mark Noll reminds the church, "Most of the things that count most about Christianity cannot be counted."[4]

YOUNG ADULTS WHO HAVE REMAINED

There are certainly some young adults who have maintained connection to the church. They appear to participate across the denominational spectrum in high and low liturgical settings: Catholic and Protestant, mainline or non-denominational, in small and large congregations. Our own research indicates that young adults self-identify certain factors that are most relevant in keeping them in the Christian community.

These factors have demonstrably little to do with denominations per se, but rather pivot around three key areas:

1. The strong sense of belonging to a family network that genuinely cares for them.
2. Opportunities for full participation in the life of the church community.
3. The belief that times of corporate worship are real, transcendent, and connected to their everyday lives.

These cannot be replicated through programming or marketing plans.

It would be foolish for a church to make overt attempts at becoming multiethnic if that was not reflected in its surrounding neighborhood. That would only communicate an inauthentic attempt to become something for its own sake. Emerging generations are wise to those ploys. However, it also makes little sense to them that people live in a diverse community and worship separately if multi-inclusive Christian community can be had.

As churches embrace the idea of becoming multi-inclusive, they must understand at the outset that working toward this takes intentionality and effort. As churches become more inclusive and their diversity increases, complexity also abounds. Intentional diversity can highlight preexisting issues of race, class, immigration status, native language, generational divides, and the like.

Certainly, people are generally more comfortable in environments where the style of leadership, modes of interaction, and topics of conversation reflect their own standards and expectations. This is even more true in the extremely personal environment of faith practice. It is therefore understandable that the development of genuine multi-inclusive Christian faith communities has not occurred quickly or easily. Greater efforts are evident in other realms such as business and education, but they don't connect with issues as deep or as personal as faith. However, the fact that change is challenging does not eliminate the need for the church to progress in this manner.

Our own journeys to reach this conclusion have taken many years and involved untold discussions, working through multiple insensitive mistakes. Through these experiences, it has become patently clear that the onus for personal and congregational transformation is not on those who are "different," but on those who continue to benefit from the power they garner as a result of their race, gender, economic status, and educational advantage. To require those being reached and served to conform to the expectations and preferences of the current racial and theological power holders is the epitome of assimilation and arrogance.

The bulk of the work to develop a multi-inclusive context rests on the shoulders of those like me (Dan) who have rarely needed to consider being the "other." It has become clear that in order to embody the work of Christ and the theology of diversity found within the Scriptures, the greatest need is that I come to experience faith through the eyes of those whose experiences are completely different from my own.

Efforts to develop more diverse Christian faith communities should not be the latest attempt at marketing to emerging generations, nor should they be interpreted as paternalistic efforts to help the poor ethnic people in the neighborhood. They also shouldn't be motivated by the desire to regain influence within a social or political arena. Emerging generations are sensitive to false advertising and gimmicks; they're generally wary of all traditional institutions and are unlikely to be convinced by grand statements or pretense. But they do retain a desire to invest in a faith community that is ready to work. This provides church members opportunities to celebrate an ever-growing understanding of God developed through interaction within the multi-inclusive community. As Soong-Chan Rah proclaims, what a purposefully diverse faith community offers everyone is the recognition that "regardless of our racial, ethnic, national, or cultural identity, we are each a spiritual image bearer of God."[5]

Those observing what was happening in the early Christian community as it exploded onto the scene had no way of describing the inclusivity demonstrated there. Men and women, slaves and free, Jew and Gentile were each accepted as equals in a manner never witnessed previously. The multi-inclusive community has always been at the center of the *missio Dei* (mission of God) for humanity, only becoming truly possible through the redeeming work of Jesus. Ultimately it will be realized through the fulfillment of the verse that we have referenced throughout this book: "a great multitude that no one could count, from every nation, from all tribes and peoples and languages, standing before the throne and before the Lamb" (Revelation 7:9 NRSV), which the author of the book of Revelation foresaw. But knowing what will happen at the end of the story should not prevent the church from pursuing that miracle in the present.

As Christians around the world pray "Thy kingdom come" in the Lord's Prayer, they're encouraged to be proactive in bringing about the necessary changes that will encourage the multi-inclusive kingdom of God. As the authors of *Neighborhood Church* declare, "If we want to enter into this 'kingdom,' this new way of being in relationship with God and each other, it requires risk and radical realignment. To say 'thy kingdom come' is a revolutionary confession of willingness."[6] Growing toward inclusivity needs to be more than simply a way to maintain the power and influence the church had in the past. It needs to reflect a willingness to become more like the early church described in Acts. Churches must be aware that unfortunately, for many, the church continues to be "more likely to reflect the individualism of Western philosophy than the value of community found in scripture."[7] If the church is to survive as the entity Jesus established it to be, then all preferential bias needs to be recognized and brought to the place of repentance. Only then can a genuinely multi-inclusive demonstration of the church take place in any meaningful way.

The divisiveness of the political arena provides little opportunity to hear the perspective of others, yet the church is one of the few places where meaningful dialogue and interaction could be taking place. In the end, the church should be the institution leading the way, demonstrating what it means to practice full love and inclusion. The response of those outside the church should be to immediately turn to the church for help when faced with issues of exclusion, injustice, bigotry, or other forms of prejudice. That is not the case now—but it should be the aim.

For the church in the future to really make connection with emerging generations, it needs to be intentional about reflecting the various perspectives these young people experience in other aspects of their lives. As Stephen Warner argues, "The key to building a congregation of people from diverse, often alienated . . . backgrounds is to appeal to them in ways that trump their differences."[8] It will be important to help them recognize that the church offers the best place to develop meaningful and long-lasting relationships with people of all ethnic, gender, cultural, generational, and familial backgrounds while at the same time working together to "incarnate their passions: passion for a just world, passion for a less judgmental church, passion for service that actually makes a difference, passion for a sustainable lifestyle."[9]

All of that will require a willingness on the part of those who retain most positions of power and influence in the church to forgo some of their comfort, relinquishing a few of their "keys," in order that a more inclusive church can develop. As Kenny Walden declares, "There needs to be a cadre of pastors and other church leaders who are willing to risk their employment, popularity, and financial security for the greater good of including all of God's creation in their faith communities."[10] There are no guarantees that the risks church leaders are willing to take will pay off with emerging generations, but many of them are already voting with their feet. If the church desires to be at the forefront of meaningful change, racial reconciliation, and empowerment of the "others" in society, then the time to act is while it retains a modicum of influence and energy to make a difference.

The future church will look different from the present church. Let us hope that all adults currently within it are concerned enough about the next generation that they are willing to engage them in ways consistent with the gospel, but free of traditions that only confirm the belief of many young adults that the church continues in its irrelevance. Perhaps, as Leon Brown exhorts us,

> As America becomes home to an even greater mix of cultures, showcasing a transcendent unity will be vital to being a compelling witness in this new, excessively diverse society. Community and unity across [multi-inclusivity] proclaims the power of the Gospel and elevates the values of kingdom culture above all competing identities and cultures. Grace will surely trump all else in such a setting.[11]

CURRENT SIGNS

Many older adults are discouraged and raise concern about the future viability of the church. Certainly, there is reason to be worried about the disconnect between emerging generations and the institutional church, in all its iterations and denominations. It should also be clear by now that though there is a growing effort in many places to develop more multi-inclusive models of church community, this is not the norm. There are still several historical and systemic impediments that prevent multi-inclusive churches from becoming the standard for church life and involvement. This should not be an excuse to give up, or to be resigned to the belief that "this is just the way things are." Simply because many have the underlying belief that "this is the way things have always been" or accept a supposed fact that "people from different cultures simply worship distinctly, and it's better that way," it does not mean things should remain in this incomplete state.

The pandemic has altered the way the church will function from now on. It is clear now that corporate worship attendance is no longer a complete means of determining the health of a congregation, if it ever was. Young people want to be engaged in change making with like-minded people. They can worship online any time they want when they need good music or a message from God. Gathering now should also happen in different ways and for different reasons. Corporate worship will always be a part of what the church does, but all the energy and resources of a church should no longer be focused on this brief weekly gathering. For people to be engaged, the church will have to make a much stronger case than Sunday morning worship for why life is more meaningful when involved with church.

Whether or not the development of the multi-inclusive church alters the trajectory of decline and launches significant numerical growth should not be the primary concern. Multi-inclusivity should be the goal because it represents a more complete reflection of the intent of God for the church and provides a powerful example for the wider society polarized by mistrust and bigotry. As Coalter wisely points out,

> It [is] important to envision an inclusive church because there are not several saviors, several salvations, or several churches offered to [people] according to their color, culture, or customs. It may be natural for like-minded people to assume their standards are the best, but it is also demonic and a blasphemy when it controls the life of the church.[12]

We know that "the homogeneous church model narrows both the Great Commission and the Gospel," as Terry Linhart attests.[13] Fulfillment of the Great Commission in an inclusive manner is the best way to broadcast to the world the realized hope of unity that the gospel promises.

Certain regions of the country clearly have greater capability to work toward becoming true multiethnic worship communities, because there is a greater diversity within the general population. But the lack of explicit ethnic diversity does not preclude efforts toward becoming multi-inclusive in keeping with the surrounding community of every congregation. Becoming multi-inclusive then becomes the intentional effort to create a space where all manner of local people feel welcome, heard, challenged, and also come to believe that they have something meaningful to offer. These are not easily measured outcomes, but no less important, and they need to be assessed in conjunction with more traditional assessments such as attendance and finances.

The primary concern of a congregation becoming multi-inclusive should be service to the surrounding community in whatever form is most needed and the church believes they are most capable of handling based on the involvement of their members. This is what the parish model encourages. Where misunderstanding between people prevails, it is often a consequence of distance, whether ideological or social. Proximity is the key to understanding; therefore, becoming immersed within the community is likely to encourage improved concord and elicit the potential for greater inclusivity within the church community. Considering surroundings as a parish generates proximate thinking. It changes the mode of engagement from seeing people in the community as a target to recognizing them as an asset that the church needs to be a better version of itself.

The change in mindset from seeing neighbors as a target to recognizing them as an asset reduces paternalistic tendencies and fosters a collaborative environment. It is often the paternalism that creates barriers for people from diverse backgrounds to becoming involved in congregations. It is wearisome to be continually subjected to the sense that they need the church for its help and support, but the church has no real need for them.

For those immersed in monocultural congregations, particularly predominantly White churches, utilizing resources, messages, studies, and special events that highlight the racial history of the church will help people gain understanding of the deep-seated nature of this issue and may begin to open opportunity for dialogue and growth. These efforts need to be consistent, as well as theologically and biblically sound, to mitigate the anticipated negative comments regarding the "political agenda" being promoted. Ultimately, it needs to be crystal clear and communicated consistently from multiple sources, including eldership, that this growth toward greater inclusivity is nothing short of fulfillment of the gospel in the local context. This is the goal in seeking to become a multi-inclusive congregation.

Ultimately the objective should be that the church encourages life in all its fullness (John 10:10) and fosters renewal in relationships between diverse people and between humanity and God. As Miroslav Volf proclaims, "The hallmark of the peace of flourishing life should be individuals and people groups truthfully reconciled to one another and living in harmony: worshiping together in the church and seeking the common good in public life."[14] That may simply be an unrealistic dream, but pursuit of that should continue regardless. The changes recommended in this book will certainly transform the church as it now exists and encourage a greater allegiance of emerging generations to enter into its work and purposes.

It makes sense that the youngest member of the emerging generations interviewed for this research have the final word. Jason Kreiss is Dan's son and was concerned to communicate that the church should be careful not to make becoming diverse a gimmick, but the church should be a genuine community of people from all walks of life. He felt it was necessary for "the church to be perceived as a community where all people were accepted, cared for, and had equal opportunities to contribute." For him this was "inclusive of ethnicity, culture, gender, or any other means of profiling."[15]

It would behoove the wider church to listen to this young voice, for he was raised in a relatively conservative theological and social context but is also embedded in emerging generations and the concomitant social understandings generated there. His cautions and desires indicate what the church will have to address. Young adults are loath to accept exclusivity for almost any reason, including ethnicity, gender, sexual orientation, or age. The segregated church may not directly cause young people to distance themselves from the Christian faith and church involvement, but, as Efrem says, "It provides them with another excuse."

FOR YOUR CONSIDERATION

Church Leader: The challenge to become a multi-inclusive community is daunting, particularly for those in leadership. But to remain a mono-cultural enclave will continue to weaken the communication of the gospel and undermine attempts to engage those within emerging generations. A multiethnic congregation may be impossible in your geographic region, but developing into a multi-inclusive community as described in this text can be a goal for all. What are some ways you can begin this process? Strategize with other leadership or other local pastors about initiating this development. Work to map out potential steps in the process and means of measurement along the way. Knowing that this will be an ongoing and dynamic development, who might be the key individuals in your congregation to help you evaluate the various processes? What markers or milestones do you anticipate seeing as your church becomes more multi-inclusive? What support will you need to maintain as you lead through this process?

Sitting in the Pew: In what ways can you help support the leadership in your congregation to encourage becoming multi-inclusive? Which of Fuller's six core commitments for engaging emerging generations do you see at work in your congregation currently? What help can you give to realize the development of some of the others? In what ways could you be involved in helping your church connect with younger and more diverse individuals? What support can you offer the leadership as this unfolds?

Millennial/Gen Z: Your perspective will be vital as the church works to become multi-inclusive. Where can you offer specific support for the process? It will likely seem slower than you might hope for and will require consistent attention and effort from a wide range of committed individuals. The involvement of those from emerging generations will be particularly important, though admittedly will not always be appreciated. How can you be intentional to connect with those from older generations and encourage them throughout the process?

All In: Consider again the six core commitments for engaging those in emerging generations. What priority would you put on each of these for your community? What are other possibilities for connecting with not only emerging generations but people of diverse backgrounds in your area? Where can you begin dialoguing with diverse communities to learn from one another and expand each other's understanding of God and humanity, in all its facets, that are the pinnacle of creation?

ACKNOWLEDGMENTS

DAN

All the "Elite 8" students and the incredible faculty: Jason Paul Swan Clark, Clifford Berger, and Loren Kerns from Portland Seminary's Leadership in Global Perspectives—this book exists because of the study, discussions, readings, blog posts, travel experiences, and prayer with all of you.

Karen Tremper and Katie Vande Brake—without your consistent encouragement and helpful editing this work would never have progressed.

Marcus, Mickensie, Pablo, Danae, Jamaal, Efrem, Darryl, Brian, Bethany, Jason—your willingness to share your reflections broadened the scope of the research and provided crucial insights that deepened this work, making it more accessible and valuable for a wider audience.

Jared, Joel, Danae, Jason, and Cindy—thank you for your constant support and encouragement throughout the entire process.

EFREM

My mentor, Dr. Robert Owens, and my spiritual father, Pastor Gerald Joiner. Your affirmations and, at times, rebukes have kept me believing in my calling as a pastor and theologian.

My parents, Forice and Sandra Smith, continue to serve as my biggest "fans." You inspire me to keep writing, preaching, and growing.

Thanks to MarkO and Dan Kreiss for inviting me to be a part of this book project. What a joy to partner with Dan.

NOTES

INTRODUCTION

[1] Kara Eckmann Powell, Jake Mulder, and Brad Griffin, *Growing Young: Six Essential Strategies to Help Young People Discover and Love Your Church* (Grand Rapids, MI: Baker Books, 2016), 16.

[2] David Crary, "Religion Remains in Sharp Decline in US," *Bristol Herald Courier*, October 18, 2019, A7.

[3] Alan Cooperman, "Religious 'Switching' Patterns Will Help Determine Christianity's Course in U.S.," Pew Research Center, September 29, 2022, www.pewresearch.org /fact-tank/2022/09/29/religious-switching-patterns-will-help-determine-christianitys -course-in-u-s/.

[4] Demographic information is based on surveys distributed and data collected during weekend worship services of Bayside Church Midtown in July of 2016.

[5] Francis Anfuso, *A City That Looks Like Heaven: Building Bridges of Unity and Love in America's Most Racially Diverse City* (Roseville, CA: The Rock of Roseville Publishing, 2014), 15.

[6] World Population Review, "Sacramento: Population," accessed April 22, 2019, http:// worldpopulationreview.com/us-cities/sacramento-population/.

1. EMERGING GENERATIONS AND THE CHURCH

[1] Kevin Ward, "Religion in a Postaquarian Age," Presbyterian Church of Aotearoa New Zealand, September 2017, www.presbyterian.org.nz/index.php/about-us/research -resources/research-papers/religion-in-a-postaquarian-age; David W. Bebbington, *Evangelicalism in Modern Britain: A History from the 1730s to the 1980s* (Milton Park, UK: Routledge, 2015).

[2] Kara Eckmann Powell, *Growing Young: Six Essential Strategies to Help Young People Discover and Love Your Church* (Grand Rapids, MI: Baker Books, 2016).

[3] Jeffrey M. Jones, "U.S. Church Membership Down Sharply in Past Two Decades," Gallup, September 12, 2019, https://news.gallup.com/poll/248837/church-member ship-down-sharply-past-two-decades.aspx.

[4]Dwight Zscheile, "Who Is My Neighbor? The Church's Vocation in an Era of Shifting Community," *Word & World* 31, no. 1 (2017): 27-36.

[5]Chap Clark, *Hurt 2.0: Inside the World of Today's Teenagers* (Grand Rapids, MI: Baker Academic, 2011).

[6]David Crary, "Religion Remains in Sharp Decline in US," *Bristol Herald Courier*, October 18, 2019, A7.

[7]Rachel Held Evans, "Want Millennials Back in the Pews? Stop Trying to Make Church 'Cool,'" *Washington Post*, April 30, 2015, www.washingtonpost.com/opinions /jesus-doesnt-tweet/2015/04/30/fb07ef1a-ed01-11e4-8666-a1d756d0218e_story .html.

[8]Powell, *Growing Young*.

[9]Kristina Lizardy-Hajbi, "Engaging Young Adults," *Faith Communities Today*, 2016, https://faithcommunitiestoday.org/wp-content/uploads/2018/12/Engaging-Young -Adults-Report.pdf.

[10]John Seel, *The New Copernicans: Millennials and the Survival of the Church* (Nashville: Thomas Nelson, 2018), xx.

[11]Crary, A7.

[12]Paula L. McGee, *Brand® New Theology: The Wal-Martization of T.D. Jakes and the New Black Church* (Maryknoll, NY: Orbis Books, 2017).

[13]Alan Cooperman, "Religious 'Switching' Patterns Will Help Determine Christianity's Course in U.S," Pew Research Center, September 29, 2022, www.pewresearch .org/fact-tank/2022/09/29/religious-switching-patterns-will-help-determine -christianitys-course-in-u-s/.

[14]Cathy Lynn Grossman, "Christians in Decline, 'Nones' on the Rise," *The Christian Century* 132, no. 12 (June 2015): 12-13.

[15]Reem Nadeem, "How U.S. Religious Composition Has Changed in Recent Decades," Pew Research Center's Religion & Public Life Project, September 13, 2022, www.pewresearch.org/religion/2022/09/13/how-u-s-religious-composition -has-changed-in-recent-decades/.

[16]Kimberly Winston, "The Rise of the Nones," *The Christian Century* 129, no. 22 (October 31, 2012).

[17]Winston, "Rise of the Nones," 14.

[18]Richard D. Waters and Denise Sevick Bortree, "Can We Talk About the Direction of This Church?" *Journal of Media and Religion*, 11, no. 4 (October 2012): 200-215, https://doi.org/10.1080/15348423.2012.730330.

[19]Seel, *New Copernicans*, 23.

[20]Seel, *New Copernicans*, 23.

[21]Seel, *New Copernicans*, 98.

[22]For the uninitiated, Burning Man is a days-long event held in the Nevada desert each year. Tens of thousands of people attend to help erect and then dismantle a temporary utopia based on the ten listed principles. It is not a festival where acts are booked to entertain attendees; rather, it is touted as a community event meant to encourage art, self-expression, and self-reliance.

[23]Seel, *New Copernicans*, 98.

[24]Seel, *New Copernicans*.

[25]Waters, "Direction of This Church," 201.

[26]Powell, *Growing Young*.

[27]Powell, *Growing Young*.

[28]Powell, *Growing Young*, 18.

[29]Krin Van Tatenhove and Rob Mueller, *Neighborhood Church: Transforming Your Congregation into a Powerhouse for Mission* (Louisville, KY: Westminster John Knox, 2019).

[30]Waters, "Direction of This Church," 201.

[31]Clark, *Hurt*, 8.

[32]Ward, "Religion in a Postaquarian Age," 6.

[33]Brian Duignan, "Postmodernism Philosophy," in *Encyclopedia Britannica*, October 2018, accessed June 23, 2019, www.britannica.com/topic/postmodernism -philosophy.

[34]Justin Nortey, "More Houses of Worship Are Returning to Normal Operations, but In-Person Attendance Is Unchanged Since Fall," Pew Research Center, August 26, 2022, www.pewresearch.org/fact-tank/2022/03/22/more-houses-of-worship -are-returning-to-normal-operations-but-in-person-attendance-is-unchanged -since-fall/.

[35]Zscheile, "Who Is My Neighbor," 30.

[36]Miroslav Volf and Matthew Croasmun, *For the Life of the World: Theology That Makes a Difference* (Grand Rapids, MI: Brazos Press, 2019), 21.

[37]Zscheile, "Who Is My Neighbor," 30.

[38]Lenny Duncan, *Dear Church: A Love Letter from a Black Preacher to the Whitest Denomination in the U.S.* (Minneapolis, MN: Fortress, 2019).

[39]Tatenhove and Mueller, *Neighborhood Church*, 4.

[40]Efrem Smith, *The Post-Black and Post-White Church: Becoming the Beloved Community in a Multi-Ethnic World* (Hoboken, NJ: Wiley, 2012).

[41]Korie Little Edwards, "The Multiethnic Church Movement Hasn't Lived Up to Its Promise," *Christianity Today*, February 16, 2021, www.christianitytoday.com/ct/2021 /march/race-diversity-multiethnic-church-movement-promise.html.

[42]James Davison Hunter, *To Change the World: The Irony, Tragedy, and Possibility of Christianity in the Late Modern World* (New York: Oxford University Press, 2010), 73.

[43]Richard Fry and Kim Parker, "'Post-Millennial' Generation On Track To Be Most Diverse, Best-Educated," Pew Research Center, November 16, 2018, www .pewsocialtrends.org/2018/11/15/early-benchmarks-show-post-millennials-on -track-to-be-most-diverse-best-educated-generation-yet/.

[44]Fry and Parker, "Post-Millennial Generation."

[45]Terry Linhart, *Teaching the Next Generations: A Comprehensive Guide for Teaching Christian Formation* (Grand Rapids, MI: Baker Academic, 2016), 125.

[46]Paul V. Sorrentino, *A Transforming Vision: Multiethnic Fellowship in College and in the Church* (South Hadley, MA: Doorlight Publications, 2011), 175.

[47]Kenny J. Walden, *Practical Theology for Church Diversity: A Guide for Clergy and Congregations* (Eugene, OR: Cascade Books, 2015), 3.

[48]Peter D. Browning, "Racial-Ethnic Diversity and the Church Related College," *Lexington Theological Quarterly* 41, no. 1 (2006): 1-22.

[49]Tori Deangelis, "Consumerism and Its Discontents," *Monitor on Psychology*, June 2004, www.apa.org/monitor/jun04/discontents.

[50]Thom S. Rainer, "5 Realities of Evangelism in North American Churches," Lifeway Research, January 26, 2023, https://research.lifeway.com/2017/10/04/5-realities -of-churches-in-north-america/.

[51]Soong-Chan Rah, *The Next Evangelicalism: Releasing the Church from Western Cultural Captivity* (San Bernardino, CA: ReadHowYouWant, 2012), 54.

[52]Kenda Creasy Dean, *Almost Christian: What the Faith of Our Teenagers Is Telling the American Church* (Oxford, UK: Oxford University Press, 2010).

[53]Christian Smith and Melinda Lundquist-Denton, *Soul Searching: The Religious and Spiritual Lives of American Teenagers* (Oxford, UK: Oxford University Press, 2011), 266.

[54]Creasy Dean, *Almost Christian*, 19.

[55]Yolanda Pantou, "Ecumenical Movement for Millennials: A Generation Connected but Not Yet United," *HTS Teologiese Studies/Theological Studies* 73, no. 1 (2017), 3, https://doi.org/10.4102/hts.v73i1.4735.

[56]Kimball, *They Like Jesus*, 18.

[57]Walden, 4.

[58]Anthony Elliott, *Contemporary Social Theory: An Introduction* (Abingdon, UK: Routledge, 2014), 7.

[59]William A. Dyrness, *Visual Faith: Art, Theology, and Worship in Dialogue* (Grand Rapids, MI: Baker Academic, 2003), 136.

[60]Rah, *Next Evangelicalism*, 1.

[61]Rah, *Next Evangelicalism*, 12.

[62]Donald M. Lewis and Richard V. Pierard, *Global Evangelicalism: Theology, History and Culture in Regional Perspective* (Downers Grove, IL: IVP Academic, 2014), 62.

[63]Megan G. Brown, "Relationships Matter: The Impact of Relationships upon Emerging Adult Retention," *Christian Education Journal: Research on Educational Ministry* 13, no. 1 (April 2016): 7-23, https://doi.org/10.1177/073989131601300102.

2. Addressing Emerging Generations Through the Multi-Inclusive Church

[1]David T. Olson, *The American Church in Crisis* (Grand Rapids, MI: Zondervan, 2008), 93.

[2]Korie L. Edwards, *The Elusive Dream: The Power of Race in Interracial Church* (New York: Oxford University Press, 2008), 98.

[3]James H. Cone, *God of the Oppressed* (Maryknoll, NY: Orbis Press, 1997), 128.

[4]Howard Thurman, *Jesus and the Disinherited* (Boston: Beacon Press, 1996), 15, 17-18.

[5]John Perkins, *With Justice for All: A Strategy for Community Development* (Ventura, CA: Regal Books, 2007), 101.

[6]Cheryl J. Sanders, *Ministry at the Margins: The Prophetic Mission of Women, Youth, and the Poor* (Eugene, OR: Wipf and Stock, 1997), 30.

[7]John Perkins, *With Justice for All: A Strategy for Community Development* (Ventura, CA: Regal Books, 2007), 90.

[8]Cone, *God of the Oppressed*, 67.

[9]Kameron J. Carter, *Race: A Theological Account* (New York: Oxford University Press, 2008), 250.

[10]Samuel George Hines and Curtiss Paul DeYoung, *Beyond Rhetoric: Reconciliation as a Way of Life* (Valley Forge, PA: Judson Press, 2000), xxii.

[11]Brenda Salter McNeil, *A Credible Witness: Reflections on Power, Evangelism, and Race* (Downers Grove, IL: InterVarsity Press, 2008), 17.

[12]Salter McNeil, *Credible Witness*, 30-31.

3. Becoming the Beloved Community for Emerging Generations

[1]Martin Luther King Jr., *A Testament of Hope: The Essential Writings and Speeches of Martin Luther King Jr.*, ed. James M. Washington (San Francisco: Harper, 1986), 87.

[2]Howard Thurman, *Footprints of a Dream: The Story of the Church for the Fellowship of All Peoples* (Eugene, OR: Wipf and Stock, 2009), 17-18.

[3]Curtiss DeYoung, Michael Emerson, George Yancey, and Karen Kim, *United By Faith: The Multiracial Congregation as an Answer to the Problem of Race* (New York: Oxford University Press, 2003), 3-5.

[4]Antipas L. Harris, *Is Christianity the White Man's Religion? How the Bible Is Good News for People of Color* (Downers Grove, IL: InterVarsity Press, 2020), 142.

[5]Mickensie Neely, personal interview with Dan Kreiss, February 11, 2022.

[6]Neely interview.

[7]*Stimming* is a term used to describe repetitive motions that help one cope with emotions. These may distract, relieve stress, or calm a person down, e.g., biting one's nails when nervous. For those on the autistic spectrum, these behaviors are often more pronounced and may be a distraction to others present in the same space.

[8]Neely interview.

[9]Neely interview.

[10]Harris, *White Man's Religion?*, 138.

[11]Bethany Fox, personal interview with Dan Kreiss, January 26, 2022.

[12]Fox interview.

[13]Andrea Perrett, "One Body, Many Abilities," *Christian Century*, February 10, 2021: 24-27, 25.

[14]Fox interview.

[15]Harvey C. Kwiyani, *Multicultural Kingdom: Ethnic Diversity, Mission and the Church* (London: SCM Press, 2020), 111.

[16]Fox interview.

[17]Harris, *White Man's Religion?*, 6.

[18]This will be discussed at greater length in chapter four, which considers the challenges to becoming multi-inclusive.

[19]Jason Clark, personal interview with Dan Kreiss, March 11, 2022.

[20]Darryl Gardiner, personal interview with Dan Kreiss, March 27, 2022.

[21]Gardiner interview.

[22]Barbara Brown Taylor, *An Altar in the World: A Geography of Faith* (New York: HarperOne, 2010), 4, 13.

[23]Jonathan Wilson-Hartgrove, *Reconstructing the Gospel: Finding Freedom from Slaveholder Religion* (Downers Grove, IL: InterVarsity Press, 2018), 142.

[24]Wilson-Hartgrove, *Reconstructing the Gospel*, 143.

[25]Francis Anfuso, *A City That Looks like Heaven: Building Bridges of Unity and Love in America's Most Racially Diverse City* (Roseville, CA: The Rock of Roseville Publishing, 2014), 15.

[26]World Population Review, "Sacramento: Population," accessed April 22, 2019, http://worldpopulationreview.com/us-cities/sacramento-population/.

[27]The House Church, "Core Values," handout at The House Church Core Team Meeting, fall 2010.

[28]House Church handout.

[29]Jamaal Williams, personal interview with Dan Kreiss, April 1, 2022.

[30]Benjamin Lindsay, *We Need to Talk About Race: Understanding the Black Experience in White Majority Churches* (London: Society for Promoting Christian Knowledge, 2019), 154.

4. The Challenges in Seeking to Become Multi-Inclusive

[1]Efrem Smith, "Crisis While the World Marches On," in *When the Universe Cracks*, ed. Angie Ward (Colorado Springs: NavPress, 2021).

[2]Michael Emerson and Christian Smith, *Divided by Faith: Evangelical Religion and the Problem of Race in America* (Oxford, UK: Oxford University Press, 2000), 21-22.

[3]Emerson and Smith, *Divided by Faith*, 25-26.

[4]Joseph Evans, *Reconciliation and Reparation: Preaching Economic Justice* (Valley Forge, PA: Judson Press, 2018), 5.

[5]Evans, *Reconciliation and Reparation*.

[6]While the "melting pot" metaphor has been used to explain the growth of the US as a land made up almost entirely of immigrants, the challenges of immigration are not only an issue within the US and its churches. To read about similar challenges in the UK and the segregation of the churches there, see the book *We Need to Talk About Race* by Ben Lindsay.

[7]We recognize that between the late seventeenth century and 1808, approximately 450,000 people were brought to North America from the African continent; but, clearly, this was not by choice and therefore not included in immigration statistics.

[8]Michael Eric Dyson, *Tears We Cannot Stop: A Sermon to White America* (New York: St. Martin's Griffin, 2021), 44-46.

[9]We believe that the terms *White* and *Black*, or even *people of color*, are racial rather than ethnic designations and therefore not particularly helpful for creating greater acceptance of diversity. But this is not an encouragement to adopt a "colorblind" ideology, as that minimizes the historical bigotry experienced by many based on race, almost universally perpetrated by those who became "White" upon immigration. We have attempted to embrace a more biblical understanding, acknowledging differences as God-ordained, through terms such as culture, ethnicity, people group, tribe, or nation.

[10]D'Vera Cohn and Andrea Caumont, "10 Demographic Trends That Are Shaping the U.S. and the World," Pew Research Center, March 31, 2016, www.pewresearch .org/fact-tank/2016/03/31/10-demographic-trends-that-are-shaping-the-u-s-and -the-world/.

[11]Cohn and Caumont, "10 Demographic Trends."

[12]Cohn and Caumont, "10 Demographic Trends."

[13]Adapted from Bryan Baker and Sarah Miller, "Estimates of the Lawful Permanent Resident Population in the United States," LPR Population Estimates, January 1, 2022, www.dhs.gov/immigration-statistics/population-estimates/LPR.

[14]Harvey C. Kwiyani, *Multicultural Kingdom: Ethnic Diversity, Mission and the Church* (London: SCM Press, 2020), 3.

[15]Kwiyani, *Multicultural Kingdom*, 4.

[16]Kwiyani, *Multicultural Kingdom*, 145.

[17]Wendell Berry, *What Are People For?* (Washington, DC: Counterpoint, 2010), 96.

[18]Emerson and Smith, *Divided by Faith*, 136.

[19]Loida Martell-Otero, "Speaking in Difference—The Church's Response to Diversity in a Globalized World," *Apuntes* 36, no. 1 (2016): 25.

[20]Emerson and Smith, *Divided by Faith*, 139.

[21]Emerson and Smith, *Divided by Faith*, 150.

[22]Jeffrey M. Jones, "U.S. Church Membership Falls below Majority for First Time," Gallup.com, May 31, 2023, https://news.gallup.com/poll/341963/church -membership-falls-below-majority-first-time.aspx.

[23]It has also likely contributed to the numeric decline of the church as people gravitated to megachurches, forcing the closure of multiple smaller congregations in much the same way that megastores like Walmart have contributed to the decline of smaller retail stores.

[24]Gary McIntosh, *The Life and Ministry of Donald A. McGavran,* referenced in Mark DeYmaz and Bob Whitesel, *Re:MIX: Transitioning Your Church to Living Color* (Nashville: Abingdon Press, 2016), 68.

[25]Mark Hearn, *Technicolor: Inspiring Your Church to Embrace Multicultural Ministry* (Nashville: B&H Books, 2017), 181.

[26]DeYmaz and Whitesel, 14.

[27]Mickensie Neely, personal interview with Dan Kreiss, February 11, 2022.

[28]Zscheile, "Who Is My Neighbor," 33.

[29]Leif Singer, "On the Diffusion of Innovations: How New Ideas Spread," accessed October 10, 2019, https://leif.me/2016/12/on-the-diffusion-of-innovations-how -new-ideas-spread/.

[30]Adapted from Singer, "Diffusion of Innovations."

[31]Singer, "Diffusion of Innovations."

[32]Rob Bell, "A Hymn for the Curve," *RobCast* podcast, episode 256, October 13, 2019, https://robbell.podbean.com/e/a-hymn-for-the-curve/. The author's interest in this theory and investigation of it came as a result of listening to this podcast by Rob Bell. It became clear that Diffusion of Innovation could be used to explain accepting the need for diversity in society in general, as well as the multi-inclusive

church movement in particular. Ideas derived specifically from that podcast are cited as such.

[33]Singer, "Diffusion of Innovations."

[34]Bell, "Hymn for the Curve." (Consider AT&T, which was one of the largest US phone companies prior to the cell phone revolution.)

[35]Singer, "Diffusion of Innovations."

[36]Neely interview.

[37]Bell, "Hymn for the Curve."

[38]Jonathan Wilson-Hartgrove, *Reconstructing the Gospel: Finding Freedom from Slaveholder Religion* (Downers Grove, IL: InterVarsity Press, 2018), 142.

[39]Kwiyani, *Multicultural Kingdom*, 76.

[40]Kwiyani, *Multicultural Kingdom*, 111.

[41]Mason Keiji Okubo, "Unity and Diversity—Being a Multicultural Church," *Concordia Journal* (Summer 2016): 203-210.

[42]Pablo Morales, personal interview with Dan Kreiss, September 17, 2019.

[43]Morales interview.

[44]Brian Butler, personal interview with Dan Kreiss, February 15, 2022.

[45]Morales interview.

[46]Bell interview. It was this interview and his comments regarding inclusion that were the catalyst for developing a new framework that incorporated all aspects of what this book seeks to accomplish. The term "multi-inclusive" developed by the authors encompasses all aspects of diversity—ethnicity, gender, culture, age, sexual orientation—and the recognition of the need for a broader term stems from this interview.

[47]Loida Martell-Otero, "Speaking in Difference—The Church's Response to Diversity in a Globalized World," *Apuntes* 36, no. 1 (2016): 25.

[48]Vibrant Congregations, "Rescuing the Gospel from the Cowboys (Part 2)," The Network, Christian Reformed Church in North America, December 16, 2021, https://network.crcna.org/church-renewal/rescuing-gospel-cowboys-part-2.

5. How the Multi-Inclusive Church Wins This Generation

[1]Charles Marsh, *Strange Glory: A Life of Dietrich Bonhoeffer* (New York: Vintage Books, 2015), 146.

[2]Jonathan Wilson-Hartgrove, *Reconstructing the Gospel: Finding Freedom from Slaveholder Religion* (Downers Grove, IL: InterVarsity Press, 2018), 86.

[3]Harvey C. Kwiyani, *Multicultural Kingdom: Ethnic Diversity, Mission and the Church* (London: SCM Press, 2020), 72.

[4]Kwiyani, *Multicultural Kingdom*, 111.

[5]Richard Twiss, *Rescuing the Gospel from the Cowboys: A Native American Expression of the Jesus Way* (Downers Grove, IL: Intervarsity Press, 2015), 29.

[6]Larry Doornbos, "Rescuing the Gospel from the Cowboys (Part 1)," The Network, Christian Reformed Church in North America, December 7, 2021, https://network .crcna.org/church-renewal/rescuing-gospel-cowboys.

[7]Carey Nieuwhof, "8 Disruptive Church Trends That Will Rule 2021 (the Rise of the Post-Pandemic Church)," CareyNieuwhof.com, February 11, 2022, https:// careynieuwhof.com/8-disruptive-church-trends-that-will-rule-2021-the-rise-of -the-post-pandemic-church/.

[8]Mickensie Neely, personal interview with Dan Kreiss, February 11, 2022.

[9]Carey Nieuwhof, "12 Disruptive Church Trends That Will Rule 2022," *Carey Nieuwhof* blog, February 11, 2022, https://careynieuwhof.com/12-disruptive -church-trends-that-will-rule-2022-and-the-post-pandemic-era/.

[10]"Top Stephon Clark Shooting Stories and Video," *Sacramento Bee*, accessed April 22, 2019, www.sacbee.com/news/local/crime/article206604044.html.

[11]City of Sacramento Police Department, *2016 Annual Report*, accessed April 22, 2019, www.cityofsacramento.org/Police/About-SPD/Annual-Report, 10-11.

[12]Jamaal Williams, personal interview with Dan Kreiss, April 1, 2022.

[13]Brian Butler, personal interview with Dan Kreiss, January 27, 2022.

[14]Mason Keiji Okubo, "Unity and Diversity—Being a Multicultural Church," *Concordia Journal*, Summer 2016: 207.

[15]Korie Little Edwards, "When Diversity Isn't Enough," *Christianity Today*, March 2021, 41.

[16]Kara Eckmann Powell, *Growing Young: Six Essential Strategies to Help Young People Discover and Love Your Church* (Grand Rapids, MI: Baker, 2016).

[17]Kristina Lizardy-Hajbi, *Engaging Young Adults*, Faith Communities Today, 2016, https://faithcommunitiestoday.org/wp-content/uploads/2018/12/Engaging -Young-Adults-Report.pdf.

[18]Krin Van Tatenhove and Rob Mueller, *Neighborhood Church: Transforming Your Congregation into a Powerhouse for Mission* (Louisville, KY: Westminster John Knox, 2019), 29.

[19]John Seel, *The New Copernicans: Millennials and the Survival of the Church* (Nashville: Thomas Nelson, 2018), 59.

6. WHOSE IDEA WAS THIS ANYWAY?

[1]Malcolm Patten, "Multicultural Dimensions of the Bible," *Evangelical Quarterly* 85, no. 3 (2013): 199.

[2]Acts 15 details a lengthy debate over the requirement for circumcision by new Gentile believers. Galatians 2 finds Paul rebuking Peter in Antioch for his inconsistent approach to eating meals with Gentiles.

[3]David Livermore, *Leading with Cultural Intelligence: The Real Secret to Success* (New York: AMACOM, 2015).

[4]Patten, "Multicultural Dimensions," 210.

[5]Patten, "Multicultural Dimensions," 198.

[6]Daniel Carroll, "Blessing the Nations: Toward a Biblical Theology of Mission from Genesis," *Bulletin for Biblical Research* 10, no. 1 (2000): 17-34, 20.

[7]Carroll, "Blessing the Nations," 20.

[8]Rolf Jacobson and Karl Jacobson, "The Old Testament and the Neighbor," *Word and World* 37, no. 1 (2017): 17.

[9]Jacobson and Jacobson, "Old Testament and the Neighbor," 572.

[10]David Smith, *Learning from the Stranger: Christian Faith and Cultural Diversity* (Grand Rapids, MI: Eerdmans, 2009), 68.

[11]Hendrik Bosman, "Loving the Neighbor and the Resident Alien in Leviticus 19 as Ethical Redefinition of Holiness," *Old Testament Essays* 31, no. 3 (2018): 579.

[12]Jacobson and Jacobson, "Old Testament and the Neighbor," 21.

[13]Jacobson and Jacobson, "Old Testament and the Neighbor," 24.

[14]One might also consider David's relationship with the Philistine king with whom he hid, the stories of Rahab and Ruth, the declarations of Kings Nebuchadnezzar and Darius regarding YHWH in the book of Daniel, and God's use of King Cyrus in restoring the Israelites to the Promised Land. All of these provide a consistent picture of God utilizing and demonstrating favor to people from other nations.

[15]Terence E. Fretheim, "The Healing and Confession of Naaman," in *First and Second Kings* (Louisville, KY: Westminster John Knox, 1999), 154.

[16]Peter J. Leithart, "2 Kings 5:1-27," in *1 & 2 Kings* (Grand Rapids, MI: Brazos, 2006).

[17]Theodore Anthony Perry, *The Honeymoon Is Over: Jonah's Argument with God* (Peabody, MA: Hendrickson, 2006), xi.

[18]Daniel C. Timmer, *A Gracious and Compassionate God: Mission, Salvation and Spirituality in the Book of Jonah* (Nottingham, England: Apollos, 2011), 22.

[19]Timmer, *Gracious and Compassionate*, 111.

[20]Walter Brueggemann, *Theology of the Old Testament*, in Patten, "Multicultural Dimensions," 199.

[21]Emerson Powery, "Under the Gaze of the Empire," *Interpretation* 62, no. 2 (2008): 134.

[22]Patten, "Multicultural Dimensions."

[23]Carson Reed, "Practical Theology in Diverse Ethnic Community: Matthew's Gospel as a Model of Ministry," *Restoration Quarterly* 60, no. 3 (2018): 167.

[24]Reed, "Practical Theology," 169.

[25] Amy-Jill Levine and Marc Zvi Brettler, "Mark 7:24-30," in *The Jewish Annotated New Testament: New Revised Standard Version Bible Translation* (New York: Oxford University Press, 2017), 75.

[26] Joseph Shulam, "Rabbis and Their Disciples Between the 1st Century B.C. and the 2nd Century A.D," *Renew*, August 28, 2019, https://renew.org/rabbis-and-their -disciples-between-the-1st-century-b-c-and-the-2nd-century-a-d/.

[27] Dorothy Weaver, "That They May All Be One: Diversity and Unity Within the Ministry of Jesus," *Vision* 11, no. 1 (2010): 13.

[28] Weaver, "That They May All Be One," 13.

[29] Lenny Duncan, *Dear Church: A Love Letter from a Black Preacher to the Whitest Denomination in the U.S.* (Minneapolis: Fortress Press, 2019), 141.

[30] Clifton J. Allen, ed., "Luke–John," in *The Broadman Bible Commentary*, vol. 9 (Nashville, TN: Broadman Press, 1973), 248.

[31] Moses Biney, "Journeying with Jesus: Discipleship in the Context of Diversity and Transnationalism," *The Living Pulpit* 23, no. 1 (2014): 17.

[32] Jacobson and Jacobson, "Old Testament and the Neighbor," 25.

[33] Jacobson and Jacobson, "Old Testament and the Neighbor," 25.

[34] Powery, "Gaze of the Empire," 137.

[35] David Gowler, "You Shall Love the Alien as Yourself: Hope, Hospitality and Love of the Stranger in the Teachings of Jesus," *Religions* 10, no. 3 (2019): 8.

[36] Smith, *Learning from the Stranger*, 68.

[37] Powery, *Gaze of the Empire,* 144.

[38] Smith, *Learning from the Stranger*.

[39] Patten, "Multicultural Dimensions," 207.

[40] Larry Hurtado, "Interactive Diversity: A Proposed Model of Christian Origins," *The Journal of Theological Studies* 64, no. 2 (2013).

[41] Smith, *Learning from the Stranger,* 142.

[42] Hurtado, "Interactive Diversity."

[43] Elizabeth E. Johnson, "Diverse Community in the New Testament," *The Living Pulpit* 3, no. 4 (1994): 20.

[44] Hurtado, "Interactive Diversity," 454.

[45] Smith, *Learning from the Stranger*, 142.

[46] Leon Brown, *All Are Welcome: Toward a Multi-Everything Church* (Oklahoma City: White Blackbird Books, 2018), 480.

[47] See 1 Corinthians 14:26, where Paul anticipates that "when you come together, each one has a hymn, a lesson, a revelation, a tongue, or an interpretation" (NRSV).

[48] Johnson, "Diverse Community."

[49] Smith, *Learning from the Stranger*, 14.

[50]Stanley Grenz, *Theology for the Community of God* (Grand Rapids, MI: Eerdmans, 2000), 466.

[51]Harry Eberts, "Plurality and Ethnicity in Early Christian Mission," *Sociology of Religion* 58, no. 4 (1997): 318.

[52]Grenz, *Theology*, 179.

7. It's Bigger Than Race or Ethnicity

[1]Stanley Grenz, *Theology for the Community of God* (Grand Rapids, MI: Eerdmans, 2000), 179.

[2]Mark DeYmaz and Bob Whitesel, *Re:MIX: Transitioning Your Church to Living Color* (Nashville, TN: Abingdon Press, 2016), 26.

[3]Efrem Smith, *The Post-Black and Post-White Church: Becoming the Beloved Community in a Multi-Ethnic World* (Hoboken, NJ: Wiley, 2012), 21.

[4]Terry Linhart, *Teaching the Next Generations: A Comprehensive Guide for Teaching Christian Formation* (Grand Rapids, MI: Baker Academic, 2016), 125.

[5]Wayne Gordon, John M. Perkins, and Richard J. Durbin, *Do All Lives Matter?* (Grand Rapids, MI: Baker Books, 2017).

[6]Marcus Bell, personal interview with authors, September 16, 2019.

[7]Jamaal Williams, personal interview with authors, October 16, 2019.

[8]Faith Formation, *Open to Wonder* podcast, Christian Reformed Church in North America, February 1, 2022, www.crcna.org/FaithFormation/open-wonder-podcast.

[9]Faith Formation, *Open to Wonder* podcast.

[10]"Pastor Demographics and Statistics," Zippia.com, September 9, 2022, www.zippia.com/pastor-jobs/demographics/.

[11]"Missions Pastor Demographics and Statistics," Zippia.com, January 2022, https://www.zippia.com/missions-pastor-jobs/demographics/.

[12]Antipas L. Harris, *Is Christianity the White Man's Religion? How the Bible Is Good News for People of Color* (Downers Grove, IL: InterVarsity Press, 2020), 78.

[13]Richard Twiss, *Rescuing the Gospel from the Cowboys: A Native American Expression of the Jesus Way* (Downers Grove, IL: InterVarsity Press, 2015), 31.

[14]Twiss, *Gospel from the Cowboys*.

[15]Miroslav Volf and Matthew Croasmun, *For the Life of the World: Theology That Makes a Difference* (Grand Rapids, MI: Brazos Press, 2019), 1.

[16]Volf and Croasmun, *Life of the World*, 6.

[17]John Perkins and Karen Waddles, *One Blood: Parting Words to the Church on Race* (Chicago: Moody, 2018), 46.

[18]We recognize that attempting to undermine the power of the racial construct in this writing and choosing to largely eliminate the use of the term *race* is a controversial

approach. The term *race* continues to be a powerful and harmful term and causes ongoing hurt and strife. Were it not for the powerful example of Dr. John Perkins, it is unlikely that we would dare to promote such a stance. However, we believe that embracing one's ethnic identity, as Perkins suggests, inclusive of Western European cultures, is a means of unifying humanity and disempowering the racial construct.

[19]Grenz, *Theology for the Community.*

[20]Grenz, *Theology for the Community*, 465.

[21]Grenz, *Theology for the Community.*

[22]Smith, *Learning from the Stranger*, 136.

[23]Grenz, *Theology for the Community*, 468.

[24]Grenz, *Theology for the Community,* 179.

[25]Mark Scandrette, *Practicing the Way of Jesus: Life Together in the Kingdom of Love* (Downers Grove, IL: IVP Books, 2011), 155.

[26]Smith, *Learning from the Stranger*, 22.

[27]Smith, *Learning from the Stranger.*

[28]Mark A. Noll, *From Every Tribe and Nation: A Historian's Discovery of the Global Christian Story* (Grand Rapids, MI: Baker Academic, 2014).

[29]Smith, *Learning from the Stranger*, 3.

[30]Smith, *Learning from the Stranger.*

[31]For a thorough understanding of these issues, see Jemar Tisby's *The Color of Compromise*; Jonathan Wilson-Hartgrove's *Reconstructing the Gospel*; Efrem Smith's *The Post-Black & Post-White Church*; and Jamaal E. Williams and Timothy Paul Jones's *In Church as It Is in Heaven.*

[32]C. S. Lewis, *The Great Divorce* (New York: HarperCollins, 1946), viii.

[33]Richard Twiss, *Rescuing the Gospel from the Cowboys: A Native American Expression of the Jesus Way* (Downers Grove, IL: InterVarsity Press, 2015), 50.

[34]Korie Little Edwards, "When Diversity Isn't Enough," *Christianity Today*, March 2021, 36-41.

[35]Edwards, "When Diversity Isn't Enough," 41.

[36]Benjamin Lindsay, *We Need to Talk about Race: Understanding the Black Experience in White Majority Churches* (London: Society for Promoting Christian Knowledge, 2019), 27.

[37]Mason Keiji Okubo, "Unity and Diversity—Being a Multicultural Church," *Concordia Journal* (Summer 2016): 207.

[38]James H. Cone, *A Black Theology of Liberation*, 20th anniversary ed. (Maryknoll, NY: Orbis Books, 1999), 59-95.

[39]Deotis J. Roberts, *A Black Political Theology*, 2nd ed. (Louisville, KY: Westminster John Knox, 2005), 219-22.

40Cheryl J. Sanders, *Saints in Exile: The Holiness-Pentecostal Experience in African American Religion and Culture* (New York: Oxford University Press, 1996), 38-48.

41Sanders, *Saints in Exile*, 19-20.

42Sanders, *Saints in Exile*, 34.

43Brenda Salter McNeil, *Roadmap to Reconciliation: Moving Communities into Unity, Wholeness, and Justice* (Downers Grove, IL: InterVarsity Press, 2015), 22.

44Salter McNeil, *Roadmap to Reconciliation*, 23.

45Samuel George Hines and Curtiss Paul DeYoung, *Beyond Rhetoric: Reconciliation as a Way of Life* (Valley Forge, PA: Judson Press, 2000), 32-33.

46Christopher W. Brooks, *Urban Apologetics: Why the Gospel Is Good News for the City* (Grand Rapids, MI: Kregel Publications, 2014), 29-81.

47Eric Mason, *Woke Church: An Urgent Call for Christians in America to Confront Racism and Injustice* (Chicago: Moody Publishers, 2018), 41-55.

48Jini Kilgore Cockroft, *From Classism to Community: A Challenge for the Church* (Valley Forge, PA: Judson Press, 2016) 11-71.

49Volf and Croasmun, *Life of the World*.

50Volf and Croasmun, *Life of the World*, 143.

51Lecrae Moore in Tisby, *The Color of Compromise*, 10.

52Cone, *Black Theology*, 11.

53Efrem Smith, *The Post-Black and Post-White Church: Becoming the Beloved Community in a Multi-Ethnic World* (Hoboken, NJ: Wiley, 2012).

8. Toward Becoming a Multi-Inclusive Congregation

1Dwight Zscheile, "Who Is My Neighbor? The Church's Vocation in an Era of Shifting Community," *Word & World* 31, no. 1 (2017): 32.

2The Fuller Youth Institute's research specifically included multiethnic and ethnic minority churches, focusing on the issue of the church growing younger in median age. While we recognize the need for the church to grow younger, the development of the multi-inclusive church will not automatically come from growing younger. However, we believe that many of the core commitments churches embrace in an effort to grow young will also help them grow to reflect their surrounding community—if they are willing to admit their cultural biases and embrace God's desire for inclusivity.

3Kara Powell, *Growing Young: Six Essential Strategies to Help Young People Discover and Love Your Church* (Grand Rapids, MI: Baker Books, 2016), 43.

4Mark A. Noll, *From Every Tribe and Nation: A Historian's Discovery of the Global Christian Story* (Grand Rapids, MI: Baker Academic, 2014), 132.

5Soong-Chan Rah, *Many Colors: Cultural Intelligence for a Changing Church* (Chicago: Moody, 2010), 27.

[6]Krin Van Tatenhove and Rob Mueller, *Neighborhood Church: Transforming Your Congregation into a Powerhouse for Mission* (Louisville, KY: Westminster John Knox, 2019), 3.

[7]Rah, *Many Colors,* 30.

[8]Stephen R. Warner, "Multiethnic Mix: A Model of Congregational Diversity?" *The Christian Century* 122, no. 15 (July 2005): 26.

[9]Tatenhove and Mueller, *Neighborhood Church,* 3.

[10]Kenny J. Walden, *Practical Theology for Church Diversity: A Guide for Clergy and Congregations* (Eugene, OR: Cascade Books, 2015), 9.

[11]Leon Brown, *All Are Welcome: Toward a Multi-Everything Church* (Oklahoma City: White Blackbird Books, 2018), chapter 13, Kindle.

[12]Milton J. Coalter, John M. Mulder, and Louis Weeks, *The Diversity of Discipleship: Presbyterians in the Twentieth-Century Christian Witness* (Louisville, KY: Westminster John Knox, 1991), 244.

[13]Terry Linhart, *Teaching the Next Generations: A Comprehensive Guide for Teaching Christian Formation* (Grand Rapids, MI: Baker Academic, 2016), 133.

[14]Miroslav Volf and Matthew Croasmun, *For the Life of the World: Theology That Makes a Difference* (Grand Rapids, MI: Brazos, 2019), 173.

[15]Jason Kreiss, personal interview with Dan Kreiss.